Gone, Just Gone

Gone, Just Gone

■ ■ ■

Thirteen Baffling Disappearances

Chris Bobonich & Harry Bobonich

ISBN 10: 1503166775
ISBN 13: 9781503166776

Contents

Also by Chris Bobonich

Plato's Utopia Recast: His Later Ethics and Politics (Oxford)

Plato's Laws: A Critical Guide (Cambridge) editor and contributor

Bloody Ivy: 13 Unsolved Campus Murders

Also by Harry M. Bobonich

Seeing Around Corners: How Creative People Think

Big Mine Run

World War II: Memories of a GI

The Great Depression

Pathfinders and Pioneers; Women in Science, Math & Medicine

Bloody Ivy: 13 Unsolved Campus Murders

For Gloria

Introduction

(Never Is a Long, Long Time)

Whenever a loved one goes missing, the family is left in agony and there is no way to describe the pain that they have to endure. The number of Americans that go missing each year is staggering, and sadly that grim fact seems to go unnoticed.

The National Crime Information Center (NCIC) is a computerized database of documented criminal justice information, which includes missing persons. During 2012, 661,593 missing person records were entered into the NCIC. That's about 1,813 adults and children that disappeared every day. By the time you read the next several sentences, one person will go missing somewhere in the country. But as of December 31, 2012, the NCIC contained only 87,217 active missing person records; the others were cleared for various reasons. ("Missing Persons and Unidentified Persons Statistics" Online article, 2012.)

The vast majority that goes missing every year are juveniles who are younger than 18 years of age. Happily, though, many of them are safely returned to their families.

Unfortunately, a small number who go missing each year are abducted or kidnapped—or vanish and are never found. These cases are the most terrifying for the families because they never have closure—only memories are left behind.

It is these disappearances that we write about in our book. We hope it will encourage those who are most vulnerable to be more pro-active regarding their own safety. We also hope that our book will remind parents to become more aware of their responsibility regarding those in their care. These hopes are for the future, but we must also remember the past. These stories help us remember those who walked away and never came back.

The District Attorney Goes Missing

Enigma

The 59-year-old, no-nonsense district attorney in quaint Bellefonte in Centre County, Pennsylvania had the reputation of being independent and tough-minded. He took on everyone, did not back down and no one got a pass.

He was dedicated to the law and fought diligently in prosecuting domestic violence and sexual-assault cases. In 1998, however, he declined to press charges against an assistant football coach at a nearby major university following allegations of sexual abuse. During his long career as a DA, he was bound to make some enemies.

The aging DA had been divorced twice and was known to enjoy the company of women. By 2005, he had decided to retire at the end of his term in December. He had been working hard and felt tired, so on Friday, April 15 he decided to take a day off from work. It was not unusual for him to get into his red and white 2004 Mini Cooper, which he loved, for a drive alone. It was one way to relieve the stress of his job as a tough, hands-on prosecutor.

On that balmy April morning he left his home, got into his car and drove northeast on a familiar but desolate road, route 192, toward Lewisburg. For some reason, he chose not to take a more direct and improved route that was available to him.

Around 11:30 a.m., after driving for a short while, he called his girlfriend and told her that he was passing through the backcountry area known as Brush Valley just northeast of the small town of Centre Hall. His last words to her were, "I love you." It was short cellphone call.

As he drove on, seemingly enjoying the day off in his beloved vehicle, he suddenly took a sharp bend in the road ahead and his sports car disappeared from view. He was never reliably seen or heard from again.

His name was Ray Gricar, and it appeared that he had mysteriously vanished into thin air or stepped off the face of the planet.

Background

Ray Gricar was born in Cleveland, Ohio on October 9, 1945. After graduating from the University of Dayton, he received his Juris Doctor degree from Case Western Reserve University School of Law in 1970. He then went to work as a prosecutor for Cuyahoga County in Ohio, specializing in difficult cases like rape and murder.

In the early 1980s, he moved to State College, Pennsylvania where he was employed by The Pennsylvania State University for only a brief time. He then accepted the position as assistant district attorney for Centre County and was elected district attorney in 1985. He served in that capacity until 2005.

Gricar married in 1969 and was divorced in 1991. He remarried in 1996 and divorced again in 2001. About a year later, he moved in with his girlfriend, Patricia Fornicola, who at the time was an employee in the Centre County district attorney's office.

He was an intensely private person and kept his emotions to himself, yet he was considered to be a charmer and a ladies' man. Gricar did, however, have a compassionate side. He was also a hard worker and spent many evenings and weekends in his office. He had high ethical standards and was keenly aware of his duty and to the responsibilities of the office he held.

It appeared to be just an ordinary pleasant spring day on April 15, 2005, when Gricar took the day off from work. His disappearance remains a riddle to this day.

It was also the year that George W. Bush began his second term as President of the United States. The Internet site YouTube went online. W. Mark Felt disclosed that he was the whistleblower in the Watergate scandal called "Deep Throat." And Hurricane Katrina viciously struck the coastal area from Louisiana to Alabama and then drenched the state of Mississippi and devastated New Orleans. Hip-hop (Kanye West and 50 Cent) and cheesy pop music (Kelly Clarkson and Gwen Stefani) dominated the music charts, and at the movies, fantasy and science fiction reigned—the leading box office hits were yet another Star Wars, the Chronicles of Narnia and Harry Potter.

He Took the Day Off

Approximately 2,000 people go missing daily in the United States. The vast majority of them, however, return home within several days. A small number tragically come to a violent end and police have the sad assignment of notifying the family. A still smaller number continue remain missing—vanishing into thin air—and Ray Gricar is one of them.

His long tenure as district attorney went well, but he was beginning to wear down, so he decided to retire at the end of his 2005 term in December. He was in good health and there were no known threats on his life, however, some of his close associates felt that something was bothering him, especially during the week of his disappearance. What was troubling the unflappable Gricar?

On Friday morning, April 15, Fornicola went to work in the district attorney's office, while Gricar chose to remain in bed. Whenever he took a day off from work, he would invariably get into his Mini Cooper and drive (He liked to drive fast) somewhere by himself. It was his way to unwind and relax from the tensions of his job. It was a balmy spring day that morning when he got dressed, but was something preying on his mind? Was the really hard-to-read district attorney troubled about some issue or was he simply looking forward to just getting away from everything for a day?

About 11:30 a.m. that morning, Gricar called Fornicola at the Centre County courthouse and told her he was driving on Route 192, heading toward Lewisburg, a town he had often visited to purchase antiques. It was a scenic drive and a road he had traveled on a number of times. He ended his conversation by telling Fornicola, "I love you." That was the last thing she would ever hear him say. ("Missing District Attorney," Sara James. Online article, May 15, 2006.)

It was late Friday night and Gricar had not returned. Fornicola waited and waited, but calls to his cellphone went unanswered. In desperation, she finally called 911 and reported him missing. When she woke up Saturday morning, it was like she had had a bad dream. The reality of it all quickly hit her—Gricar had gone missing.

Later in the evening, the police found Gricar's car in a parking lot at North Water and St. John Streets across the street from an antique market near the Susquehanna River in Lewisburg, 60 miles from his home. The only item found in his car was his cellphone. There was no forced entry or signs of foul play. There was, however, a strange finding—the police noted a strong odor of cigarette smoke when they opened his car. They also found a small amount of cigarette ash on the passenger side floor. And why was that so strange? Everyone who knew Gricar was aware that he never smoked cigarettes, but to celebrate a special occasion he would often light up a cigar. His laptop computer, which he took with him along with his wallet and keys, were missing. Gricar's car was located about 50-75 yards from the muddy banks of the Susquehanna River.

Search-and-rescue teams covered the nearby area, but did not find any telltale evidence casting light on his disappearance. There were no photos of Gricar on surveillance tapes from businesses in the surrounding area. In addition, search dogs were unable to pick up any scent of Gricar. Divers explored the Susquehanna River for any signs of him, but turned up nothing. The authorities also drew a blank when they reviewed his credit card records, bank accounts and cellphone records. Furthermore, fingerprint and DNA evidence did not provide any clues. He just vanished.

Several months later, on July 30, 2005, several fishermen found Grticar's laptop computer lodged against a support beneath the state Route 45 bridge in the Susquehanna River about 200 yards from where his car was found; however, the hard drive was missing. The police pointed out that the laptop might have been tossed from the bridge into the river.

In October, the hard drive was found in the river near a railroad bridge about 100 yards upstream from where the laptop was discovered. Unfortunately, the hard dive was so badly damaged the authorities were unable to retrieve any information from it—another dead end.

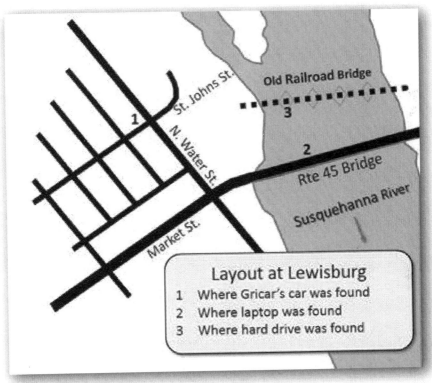

Police Officer Darrel Zaccagni, who was the lead investigator, sought the help of the state police, the FBI and the Attorney General's Office. Investigators explored every possibility but were unable to conclude definitely what might have happened to Gricar. Polygraph examinations were given to people who might have known something but nothing of interest developed from that. A number of sightings of Gricar were reported, but none of the follow-up investigations turned up results.

In April 2009, investigators revealed that someone searched the Internet looking for information on "how to wreck a hard drive," "how to fry a hard dive" and "water damage to a notebook computer" using Gricar's home computer. Was Gricar searching the Internet? Or was someone else researching for him?

But then, Gricar had made inquiries in October 2008, regarding how to erase a hard drive. "A courthouse colleague in the public defender's office told investigators that Gricar had been asking about hard-drive-erasing software as he prepared for his upcoming retirement. Maybe he was looking to clean his computer of sensitive court-related files before handing it back to the county?" ("Ray Gricar mystery: DA's privacy adds to intrigue surrounding his disappearance," Sara Ganim. Online article, *The Patriot-News,* April 15, 2012). There are, however, conflicting reports as to whether he actually purchased software to erase a hard drive.

This is suspicious behavior, especially given what happened to Gricar's hard drive. Until it can be explained, it supports the idea that Gricar intentionally disappeared.

Where was Gricar? What happened to him? There were many questions and no answers.

Theories

Suicide

In the spring of 1996, Roy Gricar, older brother of Ray Gricar, disappeared in Ohio. The police eventually found his abandoned car alongside the Great Miami River near Dayton, Ohio. Later that year, they recovered his body from the river. Roy, who had suffered from depression and bipolar disorder, had apparently taken his own life; his death was ruled a suicide.

Since the physical description of both disappearances bore some similarities, it appeared that Ray Gricar, who had some swimming capability, might have also taken his own life by jumping into the Susquehanna River. After many searches of the river by divers, boats, fishermen and also by air, as well as people walking along the banks of the river, his body was never recovered. Even to this day, no article of his clothing, his wallet or any other personal item has been found.

The ins and outs of the Susquehanna River are such, however, that under the right circumstances a body could get lodged among rocks and debris on the bottom and could conceivably never be found.

There were no indications that Gricar suffered from depression or had any medical problem, which would lead him to disappear intentionality and commit suicide. It was clear though, that there was a noted change in his demeanor several weeks prior to his disappearance.

His financial situation was sound, and he was planning for and looking forward to an early retirement. It should be noted, however, while his salary was $100,000, his assets when reviewed were rather modest. Furthermore, his Mini Cooper was titled in his girlfriend's name.

Gricar's decision to get rid of data on his laptop might simply have been to prevent others from looking at private documents. The laptop was the property of the county and would have been returned when he retired.

Is it possible, though, that he was depressed or feared some potential danger and that he did take his own life?

Walked Away

There are various reasons why people walk away, such as a secret romantic relationship, a secret behavioral problem or from some danger or a possible criminal prosecution. Some people have gone missing and managed to carry on a new life in another secluded place, even to a foreign country or a far-off island somewhere.

While it is much more difficult today to hide from the world, it can be, and has been done. Did Gricar plan the entire thing so he would not have to constantly look over his shoulder after retirement?

One possibility is that Gricar planned to meet with someone at Lewisburg who just happened to be a smoker. The arrangements were that he would then quickly leave the area in another vehicle. The smell of cigarette smoke is one of the pieces the puzzle that is hardest to accommodate on the theories of disappearance or suicide. This suggestion is the best we can do in reconciling the smoke with a voluntary disappearance. But even if Gricar had met someone to help with his disappearance (and this in itself seems unlikely), why let someone in on his movements right at the beginning of his escape? He didn't have to let him smoke in his car. If there was a smoker in Gricar's car, it seems more likely that it was a guest who wasn't welcome. At a predetermined destination, he would then travel by bus and not by air. Since he was headed for South America (he was fluent in other languages), he proceeded to travel southward to the Mexican border. He then surreptitiously crossed the porous border (no passport needed) and eventually arrived at his planned destination. This is a (barely) possible scenario.

But once you voluntarily go missing, you must stand aside and not call attention to yourself. You must give up your old ways and habits and not to be too much like your old self. It is not easy to change one's interests, hobbies and find a new career. No matter how well you plan to disappear, you always leave a trail behind.

Gricar had apparently read Pamela West's bizarre novel *20/20 Vision*, which had many details similar to his own disappearance. In West's book, the detective cleverly planned and proceeded to fake his own death. The fact that his car was found near a river echoes his brother's case, and supporters of the disappearance theory will argue that it is more likely that this was a deliberate attempt by Gricar to suggest suicide than merely a coincidental aspect of a forced abduction.

In addition, there were those who suggested Gricar had an unusual interest in the voluntary disappearance of Police Chief Mel Wiley from the outskirts of Cleveland, which occurred about five years after Gricar moved to Centre County in Pennsylvania. Were these simply matters of interest to Gricar and, therefore purely coincidental? Or was something else going on—a clue maybe?

There were sporadic sightings of Gricar after he disappeared. In some cases he was seen alone, and in others, it was reported that he was seen with a younger woman. How likely is it that he would have just walked away from everything and carry out a self-imposed disappearing act?

Gricar's family and those close to him felt that he would never have walked away. They felt that if he were alive, he surely would have contacted his family. It didn't make any sense, but stranger things have happened.

Why would Gricar with two decades in elective office, a sterling reputation, no apparent serious personal problem, a comfortable retirement to look forward to and who was planning a driving trip with Fornicola across the country just, voluntarily disappear?

The question remains, is Gricar really in hiding somewhere?

Foul Play

Gricar, a hard-driving district attorney for over three decades, handled many difficult cases. It is very likely that as an intense prosecutor he was responsible for locking away many bad guys and in doing so made some enemies. A defendant or convict might harbor a grudge for a long time, waiting patiently to seek revenge and even murder.

How probable is it that a former criminal, who Gricar had sent to prison for several years, was now trying to get even? Would he have been able to set up a meeting using by someone to lure Gricar to Lewisburg?

Furthermore, how likely is it that he could have found someone who would be willing to risk his life to help him murder Gricar? And where would he get the funds to pay someone to assist him in killing a well-known, tough district attorney?

On the other hand, let's look at another scenario. On March 31, 2005, Attorney General Tom Corbett (who later became Governor of Pennsylvania) and Centre County District Attorney Ray Gricar announced the prosecution of Taji Lee, drug cartel leader, thereby breaking up a $1.5 million heroin and cocaine drug ring.

While the case did not compare to a major drug bust in a large city, it was an important drug case and the largest carried out in the history of central Pennsylvania. Corbett thanked a number of participating police departments including Centre County DA Gricar and his agents as well as the attorneys from the Bureau of Narcotics Investigation for their extensive work in this investigation. ("AG Corbett & Centre County DA Gricar announce breakup of $1.5 million heroin & cocaine organization." Online article, Pennsylvania Office of Attorney General, March 31, 2005.)

Gricar was in the middle of this major drug investigation at the time of his disappearance. Did that cause him to be a target? Was it the prime factor in his disappearance? Just two short weeks later, Gricar went missing.

Setting a trap for Gricar, murdering him and then hiding his body mysteriously was not, however, the work of an amateur. Drug dealers are notorious for protecting their drug trade because of the huge profits to be made. They have the reputation for hiring hitmen—and we all know what they can do. Did Gricar walk into a well-planned murder trap?

The Sandusky Scandal

Jerry Sandusky served as assistant football coach for Joe Paterno at The Pennsylvania State University from 1969--1999. In 1998, the campus police investigated him after a mother claimed that he sexually molested her son in the men's shower room at Penn State. Shortly after the investigation, Sandusky retired.

In 1998, Gricar declined to press charges against Sandusky regarding the allegations of sexual abuse against him. Gricar did not have any close relationship to Penn State such as an alumnus or a football fan might have. He had, however, prosecuted people connected to Penn State in his role as district attorney.

According to reporter Christopher Moraff:

> In his defense, colleagues have insisted that if Gricar didn't move forward, it's because he didn't believe he could make a legal case for sexual abuse. A recent interview with former University Park Detective Ronald Schreffler, who investigated the 1998 case against Sandusky, sheds some light. In December [2011] Schreffler told *The Pittsburgh Post-Gazette* that the state Department of Public Welfare failed to level a charge of abuse in the case, which would have made Gricar's job difficult if he chose to prosecute anyway. ("Cops no closer to finding DA." Online article, PhillyTrib.com | *The Philadelphia Tribune*, January 15, 2012.)

In 2008, the Pennsylvania attorney general's office began to further investigate the sexual abuse allegations against Sandusky. The case soon expanded to where others also accused Sandusky of sexual abuse. The floodgates then opened and multiple allegations against Sandusky exploded anew. While there was no direct evidence suggesting any connection between the Sandusky case and Gricar's disappearance, the smoldering rumor mill went wild. But was there a connection?

In 2011, Sandusky was arrested on multiple counts of child sex abuse. In that same year Joe Paterno, Penn State head football coach, was fired and Graham Spanier, president of the Pennsylvania State University, was forced to resign. In 2012, Sandusky was sentenced to 30 to 60 years in prison. It was a bombshell that rocked the university to the core; it was the worst scandal in the history of Penn State.

Did Gricar foresee that a major scandal was brewing, which might possibly wreck his career and life? Was his disappearance somehow linked to the Sandusky case? Or is it more likely that it was just an amazing coincidence and his disappearance is unrelated to Jerry Sandusky?

Witness Protection Program

Is it possible that Gricar entered into a Federal Witness Protection Program? People so sequestered must continue on with their lives no matter where they are, however, none of Gricar's credit cards or bank accounts have been touched since he went missing.

Besides, how likely is it that the FBI would list him on their missing persons website if he was in a government protection program? More significantly, why would they continue to spend all that money and time searching for him?

At the time of his disappearance, Gricar was involved in prosecuting a large heroin drug bust. Did he receive threats against his life, which he did not reveal to anyone? On the other hand, a tough prosecutor like Gricar didn't seem to be the kind of person who would choose to be isolated from his family and society for a long time. But then, one never knows.

While the Witness Protection Program does protect a person who witnesses a crime who might be threatened by the perpetrator, it does not protect the DA who prosecutes the bad guy. Hmm. . . .

He Dropped Out of Sight

The Gricar disappearance drew national attention since it was a high profile case. His disappearance hit practically every newspaper in the country and it was all over the Internet. Major television networks showed a number of episodes featuring his bizarre disappearance. At the height of the case, most Americans had probably heard of Ray Gricar.

While there were theories and the usual rumors about his disappearance, there was very little evidence pointing to what might have happened to Gricar. While each theory had some credibility, they were not all equally probable. In essence, nothing could be ruled out.

His disappearance, however, has many followers who are intrigued by the mystery of it all. Many websites and message boards continuously review published details, and they discuss and debate the theories. (We have, in many of the cases we discuss in this book and in our previous book, _Bloody Ivy_, especially learned from the discussions on Websleuths.com.)

In October 2005, only six months after Gricar's damaged computer hard drive was found and virtually nothing else, the case appeared to begin to grow cold. While sightings of Gricar continued to be reported, none turned out to be him.

In November 2009, Stacy Parks Miller was elected as the new district attorney of Centre County.

[On March 31, 2010,] District Attorney Stacy Parks Miller has assembled a task force--comprised of former and new investigators to work the [Gricar] case. She states that after reviewing the case file & evidence that she was surprised to learn that there was much more to the past investigation than what the public was privy to— that what had been reported was only "the tip of the iceberg." She states that her personal opinion is that homicide is the least likely scenario [although she backed off that theory later] but "nothing is off the table." The fact that none of the reported witness sightings of Gricar were ever confirmed is repeated. (Timeline—Ray Gricar. Online article.)

In June 2011, Lara Gricar, Ray's daughter, petitioned for a court declaration of her father's presumed death. Centre County Judge David E. Grine approved the petition and declared Ray Gricar legally dead on July 25, 2011.

Three district attorneys have dealt with the Gricar case. In addition, two Bellefonte police chiefs and several lead detectives have also been involved.

While the Gricar case has grown cold, and he's officially dead, questions persist. Where is Ray Gricar? Is he unofficially alive? What happened? The mind-bending mystery endures.

Sorting Out the Theories

Since his brother Roy, who disappeared under similar circumstances, was later found to have committed suicide, some quickly assumed that Ray also took his own life. There was nothing, however, in Ray's background, which indicated that he had a genetic predisposition to do away with himself. After eight years, his body has never been recovered and no personal item belonging to him has ever been found. The Susquehanna is, for the most part, quite shallow, and although some have speculated there are ways in which the body may have been trapped under water, this doesn't seem very likely. Of course, it is possible that Gricar might have, for example, thrown himself down a remote abandoned mine shaft, but even if he were suicidal, why would he have wanted to cause so much trouble and heartache for his friends and family? The evidence suggesting that Ray Gricar committed suicide is weak, and there is no factual basis to support the theory that he ended his own life.

When the Sandusky sexual abuse case broke wide open, many quickly linked Gricar's disappearance to his case. In 1998, Gricar felt that there was insufficient evidence to press charges against Sandusky following allegations of sexual abuse against him.

> Bellefonte police Detective Matthew Rickard told the Associate Press that he's planning to review former Centre County District Attorney Ray Gricar's handling of the allegations against Sandusky 13 years ago—just to be thorough.
>
> Rickard, the lead investigator in Gricar's disappearance said, "There is no evidence or anything that has ever come to my attention that in any way suggests the Sandusky investigation had anything to do with the disappearance of Ray Gricar." Nonetheless, "I'm looking into that, I guess, for my own curiosity . . . but I don't expect this to lead to anything." ("Ray Gricar's disappearance likely not linked to Jerry Sandusky case, investigators say." Online article, November 11, 2011.)

While the Sandusky case adds to the intrigue surrounding Gricar's disappearance, there just isn't any evidence that the two cases are linked.

The Witness Protection Program is basically for witnesses who are seeking protection for crucial information they could provide to the authorities in a specific and important case. Gricar did not seem to be the "essential witness" the government needed to prosecute anyone. Furthermore, he was also not the type of person who would choose to enter such a program.

It is also unlikely that the government would get involved in such a high profile case and deceive the public, spending time and money by hiding Gricar away in a protection program for years.

Gricar could have voluntarily walked away. While there was evidence that he arrived in Lewisburg, there are no records, sightings, leads or anything else showing that he left town on his own. Perhaps the strongest reason for thinking that he disappeared of his own accord is that we might well think that if he was searching for information about erasing a hard drive, he was likely to have tossed his laptop into the river himself. It seems a strange coincidence that he would voluntarily throw his laptop into the Susquehanna River in about the same place and at the same time that someone else was about to abduct him.

His disappearance was a notable case and received national media coverage. The world isn't as large as it once was, and with modern technology, it would have been very difficult for him to go unnoticed for years. Furthermore, there were no reliable sightings of him since he went missing.

His interest in some people who have successfully disappeared (fiction or otherwise) is more likely a fanciful notion rather than anything serious he would have carried out. Moreover, he needed money to live and where was that coming from? Besides, there was no indication that he had a secret life out there somewhere.

But then, it does happen that some people voluntarily decide to disappear and start a new life. In doing so, however, it often involves money matters such as a large debt, a crumbling relationship, a looming personal danger or a scandal of some sort.

He seemed to have everything to live for, no health problems, no financial worries and no serious matter related to his duties as a district attorney. Gricar could have retired comfortably at the end of the year and do almost anything he wanted.

While walking away is more probable than the three theories just discussed (suicide, the Witness Protection Program and the Sandusky case), it does not appear very likely that Gricar would have simply walked away from his family and the comfortable life he was leading at the time he went missing.

Scenario for Gricar's Demise

One of the things that make the Gricar case so fascinating is that the evidence points in different directions. We think the most important considerations are the following:

(1) since the disappearance, there has been no sign of Gricar dead or alive,

(2) the strange presence of cigarette smoke in Gricar's car, and

(3) the discovery of Gricar's hard drive in the river after he had searched for information about how to destroy a hard drive.

The absence of a body points strongly away from suicide, and we think it is the least likely option. (3) does point away from the idea of murder, and a voluntary disappearance is a reasonable possibility. (We do offer an explanation of (3) below.) But we also think that (1) and (2) outweigh (3) and that the most likely scenario is that Gricar was the victim of foul play. Also, supporting the idea of foul play is the fact that those closest to him, although they did detect signs of anxiety, thought that Gricar was not showing symptoms of the sort that might lead to suicide or escape. This has some weight, but it is hard to know the heart of another person and Gricar was an intensely private individual.

If Gricar planned to disappear, it seems likely that he would have chosen a more suitable time to arrive in Lewisburg than over the noon hour, since he had visited there often and was readily recognized. Furthermore, it would have taken him considerable time to dispose of the hard drive and laptop considering where they were found, and therefore, several people probably would have seen him. Why not arrive in Lewisburg at night and immediately get into another vehicle and vanish? We feel this point also lends credence to foul play.

So here is our best idea of what happened when Gricar went missing. He had apparently planned to meet someone in Lewisburg on that Friday he took off from work. It's likely that the meeting was related to the anxiety he showed over the past several weeks. As shrewd as Gricar was, he was not aware that he was being set up and lured into a trap—probably by a femme fatale. While he intended to return home that night or sometime over the weekend, it turned out to be a meeting for murder.

In his role as a tough district attorney, Gricar clearly made some ene-mies. A former amateurish criminal, who had been sent to prison by Gricar and was now seeking revenge, could not have easily murdered him.

It was, however, a well-calculated killing by two professional hit-men who were hired by the drug cartel. The seductress first met with Gricar in Lewisburg in a parking lot across the street from an antique market not far from the Susquehanna River. It was the same location where the authorities found his car the day after he disappeared. The initial meeting took place in Gricar's car where the woman not only talked, but also smoked and left some cigarette ash on the passenger side floor. She, and the two hit men, were careful not to leave any fin-gerprints behind.

While Gricar had apparently searched the Internet on how to wreck a hard drive in a computer, he did not take his laptop along specifically for that purpose. There was no pressing need for him to carry out that task in Lewisburg since he had eight months to work on that before he retired. While he most likely would have destroyed the hard drive at some point, he would have returned the government-issued laptop.

When the killers showed up at the parking lot, they quickly took note of the laptop in his car. After a short while, one of the hit men removed the hard drive, which he then carried along with the laptop to a nearby railroad bridge. He tossed the hard drive into shallow water not far from the bank of the river. Then he continued walking a little farther on the railroad bridge and threw the laptop into the river where the water was deeper and also flowing more swiftly.

Several months later, divers found the laptop lodged against one of the concrete supports on the north side of the state Route 45 Bridge about 100 yards downstream from where it was thrown into the river.

The evidence that the laptop might have been tossed into the river from the state Route 45 Bridge is very weak. The walkway was on the south side of the bridge and not on the north side. It would have been sheer folly for someone to use the footbridge, cross over two lanes of traf-fic and toss the laptop over the north side railing into the river and then cross back over two lanes of traffic again. Why not just toss the laptop over the south side?

On the other hand, one could propose that the laptop was thrown over the bridge from a car. In that case, the car would have to slow down appreciably, or more likely stop for a brief period, for someone on the passenger side to get out and toss the laptop over the railing into the river. But the major problem with that suggestion is the car would have to be traveling into Lewisburg and in the direction toward Bellefonte. A car using the bridge to leave Lewisburg would have to travel in the south lane.

A few months after the laptop was found, the hard drive was discovered embedded in some debris in about three feet of water. The hard drive was relatively close to the bank of the river and not too far from the railroad bridge from which, it was likely tossed.

The killers were in control of the situation, and with their weapons handy, they were able to persuade Gricar to enter their vehicle. They drove off with their captive to a preplanned remote location where they quickly murdered him. It was all over very fast.

They proceeded to hide his body close to the killing site where it most likely will never be found. It was a professional murder that was well planned from beginning to end.

If you have any information about this case, which you feel might be helpful, please call the Bellefonte Police Department at 814-353-2320.

Updated Claim—Gricar was Murdered

In May 2013, a source described as a ranking official of the Hells Angels biker gang told the *Altoona Mirror* that a former member (call him Mr. X) was responsible for the murder of Ray Gricar. The source requested that the paper not reveal the identity of Mr. X.

The source stated that Mr. X did so to get even with Gricar for the harsh sentence he received for aggravated assault in the late 1990s. He said that Mr. X had also worked as an informant while he was a Hells Angel in the early 1990s.

After checking the Centre County files, the *Altoona Mirror* was able to confirm that M. X was convicted of aggravated assault, received a multiple-year prison term and had worked for the FBI while a member of the Hells Angels in the early 1990s.

A letter from the FBI to the Centre County Judge who presided over the aggravated assault case in the late 1990s was read aloud during a sentencing hearing and indicated the man [Mr. X] had provided FBI with intelligence regarding the illegal activities of outlaw motorcycle gangs after his release from federal prison after serving five years of a 12-year sentence. ("Police probe claim Gricar killed," Greg Bock Online article, *Altoona Mirror*, September 20, 2013.)

The source said that he spoke out because he thought that Mr. X was dead. Investigators, however, learned that he was living in another state.

The source said that while he started out to take the FBI agents to the exact location of the shaft where Gricar and four others were deposited, he changed his mind. He also said that Gricar's "knee caps were spun" and that his throat was slit prior to dumping him in a shaft, which is now covered with dirt.

He said that he decided not to identify the location of the shaft since it might incriminate him in the other cases. Furthermore, he said that he didn't have immunity from prosecution regarding any evidence that might be discovered in the shaft.

Bellefonte police Chief Shawn Weaver told the *Altoona Mirror*, September 22, 2013, that there's a one percent chance a former Hells Angel is behind the murder of Ray Gricar. Weaver said, "We looked into the claim thoroughly, and there may be some loose ends, but at this point, it is unsubstantiated." ("Bellefonte chief doubts Hells Angels Gricar story," Greg Bock. Online article, *Altoona Mirror*, September 22, 2013.)

Mr. X may have had motive and opportunity and was probably capable of murder. But unless the source leads authorities to the bodies, this is one more fascinating blind alleys in the Gricar case.

Another Gricar Update

It is now nine years and counting: the Gricar case still remains unsolved. In February 2014, the Pennsylvania State Police announced that they were the new investigative team in the Gricar case, taking over the reins from the Bellefonte Police Department. "Our investigators are looking at any leads and re-interviewing everyone. If it leads to something more we'll continue to follow up on it," said Jeff Petucci, State Police Trooper. Since taking over, the state police have reported that they have received a number of new tips from the hotline 800-472-8477. The police did not comment on the nature of information received.

When reporter Jennifer Miller contacted Gricar's daughter, Laura, she chose not to be interviewed. ("Still No Answers 9 Years After District Attorney Ray Gricar Disappeared," Jennifer miller. Online article, State College.com, April 15, 2014.)

Recommended Reading

Timeline—Ray Gricar. Online article, March 31, 2010.

Ray Gricar was not the only prosecuting attorney to come to a puzzling fate in central Pennsylvania. Only five years after Gricar's disappearance, Jonathan Luna died under truly mysterious and weird circumstances. As you'll quickly see, this is not a story of a disappearance, so we're presenting it as an addendum to the tale of Ray Gricar. But as we hope you'll agree, the story is just too intriguing for us to pass up and not retell.

The Last Midnight Ride

Luna's Curious Leaving

A young Assistant United States Attorney, Jonathan Luna, was working late in his courthouse office in Baltimore on the night of December 3, 2003, when he abruptly left the building. Shortly before midnight, he mysteriously drove away without any explanation, leaving behind his eyeglasses, which he needed to drive and his cell phone. At the time, he was working on a difficult plea agreement favorable to the defendants, which he also left behind and unfinished.

Luna went on a wild six-hour midnight ride in his silver Honda Accord. EZ pass records and toll tickets showing him driving through four states going from one turnpike to another documented his route. When he finally exited the Pennsylvania Turnpike at 4:04 a.m., there was a spot of blood on his toll ticket.

Shortly before dawn, Luna's car was found still idling with the front end nosed down into a cold December stream near the small town of Denver, Pennsylvania, about two miles from the exit of the turnpike. There was some blood smeared across the door on the driver's side, as well as on the left front side of the car. A small pool of blood was also discovered on the back seat floor. Loose paper currency of various denominations was scattered about inside the vehicle. Luna's dead body was found face down in the icy stream beneath the engine of his Honda. He was stabbed 36 times.

Some wounds were deep and severe, but many were shallow stabbings, which are also called "hesitation" wounds.

Where was he going? Whatever happened and why?

Background

Jonathan Luna was born on October 21, 1965, and was of African-American and Filipino ancestry. He was reared in a rough and tumble neighborhood in the South Bronx, and saw violence and drug peddling on the streets from an early age. To his credit, he eventually graduated from Fordham University and also the University of North Carolina law school at Chapel Hill.

He worked for the Federal Trade Commission for several years and also as a prosecutor in Brooklyn before accepting the position as Assistant United States Attorney in Baltimore.

Luna's wife, Angela, was an obstetrician-gynecologist, and they had two children.

Plea Agreement Dilemma

On December 3, 2003, Luna was in the third day of a trial, however, he had less than 24 hours to live. He was prosecuting Deon Smith, 32, and Walter Poindexter, 28, who were involved in the sale and distribution of heroin.

At this point, the trial started to go badly for Luna. His chief witness, Warren Grace a convicted heroin dealer, was a paid FBI informant who reneged on the conditions of his confidential informant program. This turn-about by Grace caused a serious problem for Luna. He had no choice but to offer a plea bargain to the defense, which he did over the lunch break.

In his excellent book, *The Midnight Ride of Jonathan Luna*, William Keisling wrote:

> That plea agreement, Luna knew, could not be lawfully completed. The plea agreement, Luna knew, would unlawfully cover up a murder he was obliged to prosecute: Walter Poindexter's murder of Alvin Jones.

> Trouble was, Luna was under tremendous pressure to complete the plea agreement, despite the law.

> If he did not find a way to complete the plea agreement, Luna and his fellow conspirators working in law enforcement would in a day or two find themselves under investigation in federal court.

Keisling pointed out that Grace, who supposedly was under house arrest, was allowed to move about as he pleased and even testified that he purchased heroin with Smith and Poindexter.

The defense team immediately accused Luna of failing to make proper disclosures prior to the trial regarding Grace's highly irregular interactions with the government. Judge William Quarles Jr. then agreed to investigate Luna and his FBI associates.

Luna quickly agreed to a plea deal, halting the trial, as well as the inquiry of himself and the FBI.

According to Keisling:

> Luna offered a plea agreement that knocked decades off Smith and Poindexter's jail time. In addition, Poindexter wouldn't be charged with Alvin Jones' murder. Trouble was, the agreement wasn't legal.

> A young assistant U.S. attorney [Jonathan Luna] in [U.S. Attorney Tom] DiBiagio's office, responsible for Warren Grace, suddenly found himself sitting on a political scandal of the first

magnitude. He would now have to cover it all up. To protect himself. To protect his boss. To protect the FBI.

Nevertheless, Luna stated in court that he would finish writing the plea agreement and fax it to the defense attorneys that night for them to review, which he failed to do. He was, however, also scheduled to appear in court the next morning at 9:30 a.m. for the end of the trial.

Shortly before midnight, Luna suddenly left his courthouse office, but did not drive south toward his home. Instead, for some strange reason, he drove out of Baltimore and headed northeast. It turned out that he went on a death ride.

But what was the unexplained journey all about?

The Fatal Six-Hour Timeline

The following timeline describes what was going during those last hours of his life.

11:38 p.m. Luna left the courthouse, and headed northeast on I-95 using his E-Z Pass going to Delaware. He drove relatively fast as if he had a purpose in mind.

12:57 a.m. Someone withdrew $200 from Luna's bank account at an ATM in Newark, Delaware. Security cameras were not working to capture an image.

02:37 a.m. Luna entered the New Jersey Turnpike, but there was a one hour time gap from the time he left Newark. Did he meet with someone?

02:47 a.m. He crossed the Delaware toll bridge and accessed the Pennsylvania Turnpike.

03:20 a.m. Luna's debit card was used to purchase gas at the King of Prussia Service Plaza. The security cameras were unable to capture any images.

04:04 a.m. Luna's car exited the turnpike at the Reading/Lancaster interchange. The toll ticket has a spot of blood on it. Was it Luna's blood or was someone sending a message?

05:30 a.m. Luna's Honda was discovered off Dry Tavern Road in Denver, Pennsylvania, with the front end headed downward in a cold stream. His body was found with his face down beneath the engine of his car. He had been stabbed 36 times. (According to William Keisling, *The Midnight Ride of Jonathan Luna.*)

Luna's Controversial Death

After Luna left the Pennsylvania Turnpike, his car ended up in a desolate area about two miles away at the Sensenig & Weaver Well Drilling Company on Dry Tavern Road, in Denver, Pennsylvania. While there were several twisting roads from the turnpike to that remote region, none of them were easy to navigate at that hour. (Google Sensenig & Weaver Well Drilling, Denver, PA, for a map of the area.)

Daniel Gehman, an employee of Sensenig & Weaver, arrived at 05:00 a.m., but did not see Luna's car. At 5:30 a.m., however, he noticed a small red light glowing from the dashboard of his car at a nearby stream. When he went to investigate, he assumed that it was a car accident and called 911. The state troopers arrived at 5:45 a.m. Luna's Honda was found with the motor was still idling, the lights were off, but the front end was nosed down in a shallow icy stream. His body was found face down in cold water and under the car engine. He was fully clothed with his electronic security pass around his neck, but his wallet was missing.

The front left of the car and the door on the driver's side was stained with blood. A small pool of blood was found on the back seat floor, which was odd. Loose paper currency of various denominations were scattered about inside the vehicle. While some DNA and fingerprint evidence was collected, the authorities were unable to find a match with a potential suspect. (William Keisling, *The Midnight Ride of Jonathan Luna.)*

At 08:05 a.m., Lancaster County Coroner Dr. Barry Walp pronounced Luna dead at the site. Luna had been stabbed 36 times in the throat and neck area with his personal penknife. Walp, however, stated that the cause of death was due to drowning. [The word penknife originally came from a knife that was used to thin and point quills for use in writing instruments, as well as for repairing or re-pointing the quills. The first known use of the word, was between 1400-50; late Middle English.]

Several hours later, Dr. Wayne Ross Lancaster County Forensic Pathologist, also examined Luna and noted a traumatic injury to the right side of Luna's head.

The Sensenig & Weaver Well Drilling Company was located out in the countryside close to a rural road. It had a warehouse building with a parking lot behind it where it stored industrial equipment. The authorities pointed out that tire tracks, which Luna's car left on the frost covered ground indicated that it was parked at the rear of the Sensenig & Weaver property for a time, before it was driven into a nearby stream.

At first the FBI reported that many of the stab wounds were minor and shallow. They also pointed out that there were no substantial defensive wounds on Luna's hands. The penknife was found lying next to a rock in the water near his body two months later, but did not have any fingerprints on it. The authorities felt that the wounds were self inflicted and leaned toward calling Luna's death a suicide.

Coroner Walp, who performed the autopsy, reported that Luna's death was a homicide. He stated that his hands had knife wounds, and that there were significant cuts to the throat and scrotum. Dr. G. Gary Kirchner, who succeeded coroner Walp, also confirmed that Luna's death was a homicide. ("Witness: Luna stabbed in back, his hands and scrotum slashed," Online article, yardbird.com, November 19, 2006.)

When Keisling interviewed Kim MacLeod, the undertaker who embalmed Luna, she stated that Luna's hands had been shredded. She went on to say they were defensive wounds incurred trying to defend off his attacker. MacLeod also stated that Luna had been stabbed in the middle of his back.

Theories

Suicide

Shortly after Luna's death, a number of stories circulated suggesting that he might have led a double life. The stories were an attempt to defame his character by citing some troubling issues Luna had in his financial and professional life.

Some suggested motives supporting the suicide theory: (1) He had a credit card debt, of $25,000; however, Keisling wrote that Luna's wife reported that it was $17,677; (2) He had other credit cards, some of which his wife, Angela, was unaware of; (3) His name was listed on an Internet dating site; (4) He was scheduled to take a polygraph test regarding $36,000, which mysteriously disappeared from a bank robbery case that he prosecuting; (5) It was speculated that he was trying to fabricate a kidnapping and attack, but that it spun out of control; and (7) Many of his stab wounds were shallow pin pricks referred to as "hesitation wounds" in a suicide victim. (Jonathan Luna - Wikipedia, the free encyclopedia.)

On December 3, 2003, when Luna left his office he was working on an awful plea agreement that he felt he could not complete satisfactorily, and therefore left unfinished. What role did the troublesome plea agreement play in his disappearance?

Homicide

Coroners' Walp and Kirchner both attested to the fact that Luna's death was a homicide. They specifically addressed the deep stab wounds to Luna's body and the multiple defensive wounds on his hands and fingers.

"Kirchner, who took office as coroner January 2004, confirmed reports that he was approached by FBI agents and asked to change the ruling of his predecessor, veteran coroner Dr. Barry Walp, and the county's forensic pathologist, Dr. Wayne Ross, who had determined that Luna died by homicide. But Kirchner said he agrees with the findings and won't change the conclusion of the autopsy report." ("The Curious Case of Jonathan Luna," by Helen Colwell Adams. Online article, Updated October 2, 2008.)

Keisling supports the theory that Luna was murdered. He posited that Luna might have been left for dead in his car at the rear of the Sensenig & Weaver property. Luna, though seriously injured, somehow was then able to drive his Honda a short distance into the creek. He managed to leave his car, but then wobbled, stumbled and fell headfirst down into the stream.

But who would want to kill him in such a vicious manner?

Somebody Knows Something

Luna's supporters are still seeking answers even though the Justice Department inspector general has turned down a request to investigate the case in 2005.

In 2007, Luna's family hired an attorney and a private investigator who filed a petition attempting to force the Lancaster County coroner to conduct an inquest into his death, even after a previous request was denied.

To this day, Jonathan Luna's death, at age 38, remains an unsolved mystery.

Luna's Perplexing Murder

Jonathan Luna's death remains a tantalizing mystery. It is true that at the time of his death, his personal and professional lives were in chaos and this may have caused have caused him to take extreme steps. If it was suicide, the wounds inflicted were prolonged and painful, and since he died of drowning, the stabbings were not directly fatal. (It would be interesting to know whether alcohol or drugs were found in his system. If they were, they were perhaps signs that he was trying to overcome his natural instincts to self-preservation.) It also is difficult to explain, on the suicide theory, why he went on a wild ride and wound up in such a desolate area. And why withdraw $200 in cash if you intend to kill yourself?

More probable is that he was trying to fake an attack that might have won the sympathy of his wife and those who were investigating him. Many of the wounds were not serious, and could have supported the cover story that he was attacked. The $200 might have been intended to prop up the claim that his attackers tried to rob him (although it would have been better to dispose of the cash, and say that his attackers took it than to scatter it around the car.) Maybe a few of the wounds went further than intended, and he just collapsed in the stream.

But ultimately we think that the most important evidence is that provided by the coroners. The only medical expert who actually examined the body thought it was a murder, and this finding was reaffirmed by his successor. We think this direct evidence must outweigh contrary speculations about the other truly bizarre features of the case. Somebody—at least up to now—has gotten away with murder. We just don't know who and we don't know why.

If you have any information about this case, which you feel might be helpful, please call the FBI at 410- 265-8080; or the toll free hot line number at 1-800-332-6039.

Jonathan Luna's Death and Ray Gricar's Disappearance

Some similarities for the reader to think about, both:

1. Were prosecutors.
2. Appeared to be troubled about some issue before disappearing.
3. Apparently left alone, and drove away.
4. Left some personal items behind, namely a cell phone and laptop.
5. Might have been lured to a meeting of some sort.
6. Might have been murdered or committed suicide.

7. Were involved with heroin drug dealers. Luna was prosecuting a case against two heroin dealers, when he suddenly vanished from his courthouse office. Gricar, on the other hand, was in the midst of breaking up a known heroin drug ring when he disappeared.

Are these similarities meaningful and connected? Or are they just coincidences?

Recommended Reading

Adams, Helen Colwell, "The Curious Case of Jonathan Luna," Online article, Updated October 2, 2008.

Keisling, William. *The Midnight ride of Jonathan Luna*, Harrisburg, PA. Yardbird Books, 2004 – 2008.

The Doctor Disappears the Day the
Buildings Came Tumbling Down

Last Seen the Day Before

Late in the afternoon on 9/11, a gray pall of cloud hung over lower Manhattan. It was not an unusual weather phenomenon, but the result of a diabolical terrorist attack on the World Trade Center. It was a day most Americans can remember where they were when they heard the unbelievable news that the Twin Towers were brought down. To those who were there, it was Armageddon.

It was the deadliest attack on United States territory in history. In total, approximately 3,000 people died in the attacks, and hundreds of people were reported missing to the police.

In 2001, George W. Bush was sworn in as the 43rd president. Wikipedia, the free encyclopedia, was launched. Apple brought out its iPod. And an earthquake measuring 7.9 on the Richter scale killed at least 20,000 and injured 167,000 people in India.

On the previous day, Doctor Sneha Anne Philip had the day off from her internship duties at St. Vincent's Medical Center on Staten Island. Ronald Lieberman, her husband, also a physician, was serving his internship at Jacobi Medical Center in the Bronx. About midafternoon, Philip had a two-hour online talk with her mother. She was last seen that evening by a department store surveillance camera not far from her apartment. She was also only several blocks from the World Trade Center.

Philip did not return to their residence that night, and when Lieberman woke up early the next morning his wife had still not returned. That evening after the terrorist attacks, she still had not returned to their apartment. She did, though, leave most of her credit cards, passport and other personal identification at home.

A videotape of a woman that resembled Philip was recorded on a security camera in their apartment lobby shortly before the first plane hit the North Tower. The woman paused near the elevator for a minute and then turned and left the building. The image was blurred due to the angle of the sun, so Lieberman was unable to positively identify the bleached image as his wife.

If it was Philip, or if she were somewhere else in the vicinity of the World Trade Center, did she rush to help those in need of aid? Her body was never recovered, but did she really perish in the rubble of the Twin Towers along with hundreds of others?

When the police investigated Philip's disappearance, they found that she had shown a pattern of risky behavior in her personal and professional life. This startling revelation led them to suggest that she might have met a different fate.

Since the city was in chaos, did Philip choose the attack as a time to disappear and start a new life and another identity? Did she, overwhelmed by the chaos of her life, commit suicide? Or did she encounter some evil person who ended her life the night before?

Her disappearance is still a mystery to this day.

Background

Sneha Anne Philip was born on October 2, 1969 in the state of Kerala, located in the southwest region of India on the Malabar Coast. When she was a child, her parents moved to upstate New York, settling in the small town of Hopewell Junction.

After graduating from Johns Hopkins University, she was admitted to the Chicago School of Medicine in 1995 where she met her future husband, Ronald Lieberman. They both graduated from medical school in 1999 and several years later they were married in upstate New York.

Philip was five-six, 115 pounds and 31 years old. She was attractive with an engaging smile. Philip had black hair, a small mole on her left cheek and piercing friendly brown eyes. She turned heads in a way, because she seemed too young to be a doctor. According to her eldest brother, Ashwin Kochiyil Philip, Sneha "was a classical musician, writer and artist. She had the sense and ethos of a creator."

Following their marriage, the couple moved to New York City where Philip did her internship at the Cabrini Medical Center, which was relatively close to their apartment, while Lieberman's internship was at Jacobi Medical Center in the Bronx.

During the spring of 2001, Philip's disturbing personal behavior was seriously affecting her professional career. The Cabrini Medical Center did not renew her internship because she reported late for work repeatedly and also had severe alcohol-related problems.

Philip was annoyed by Cabrini's action and went to a bar with some Cabrini employees that night. She got into a dispute and ended up spending the night in jail. It turned out that she was charged with making a false complaint (a sexual abuse charge) against a fellow intern.

More significantly, she continued frequenting lesbian and gay bars and also staying out all night. Even though she received another internship at St. Vincent's Medical Center, her indiscretions continued. Before too long, she was suspended from her internship for missing a meeting with her substance-abuse counselor ("Sneha Anne Philip," Online article, Wikipedia – the free encyclopedia).

On Monday, September 10, the last day she was seen, she had been formally arraigned for filing a false complaint against a colleague. After the hearing, she and Lieberman had quarreled at the courthouse. She walked away while he went to their apartment and prepared to go to work.

Philip had the day off. It was also the day she vanished.

Nowhere to Be

After the spat with her husband at the courthouse, Philip went home. Around midafternoon she called her mother and had a two-hour conversation with her. She left her apartment at about 5:15 p.m. and went shopping at Century 21, a discount department store close to the World Trade Center. She purchased lingerie, pantyhose, a dress and some bed linens. Then she went to a store next door and bought three pairs of shoes. At 7:18 p.m., a security camera at Century 21 recorded Philip during her shopping trip. A clerk at Century 21 said that she saw Philip shopping with another young woman, probably of Indian descent, but she was never identified ("Last Seen On September 10th," by Mark Fass. On line article, June 26, 2006).

On the night of September 10, Lieberman was home alone when someone made a call from his apartment to his cell phone at 4:00 a.m. He stated that he didn't remember making the call, but he thought that perhaps he awoke, and while still half asleep, checked his voicemail.

When Philip did not return home that night or the next morning, Lieberman was both annoyed and worried. He felt, however, that she might have stayed with some friends or with her brother, John, as she sometimes did.

Lieberman awoke early that day and headed off to work since he had an 8:00 a.m. meeting that morning. When he left the meeting about an hour later, he quickly learned that an airplane had struck the North Tower of the World Trade Center only several blocks from their apartment.

There was so much confusion going on at Ground Zero that Lieberman was not able to find out anything about his missing wife. The police were overwhelmed with reports of missing people, and at first, they assumed that Philip had likely perished in the attack. The next day, Lieberman filed a missing person report.

Lieberman, who was quickly cleared as a suspect, realized that the police had their hands full and could not immediately carry out a full-scale search, so he decided to hire Ken Gallant, a former FBI agent, to search for his wife. Lieberman, Philip's family and friends also began circulating flyers in an attempt to see if anyone was able to provide any information about her whereabouts.

Gallant did uncover a grainy videotape of a woman who resembled Philip on the security camera in their apartment lobby just prior to the attack on the World Trade Center. The woman stood near the elevator for a short time and then turned around and left the building. Lieberman was unable to positively identify the person as his wife due to the poor quality of the image.

Gallant did not find anything on Philip's computer that would lead him to think that she planned to disappear voluntarily. The fact that she left behind her glasses, driver's license, passport and credit cards, except for her husband's American Express card, suggested that she did not intentionally disappear. He also talked to Philip's friends, went to bars she frequented and visited stores where she shopped but was not able to uncover information much that was not already known. Furthermore, the two shopping bags that Philip was seen carrying were not found in her apartment.

The police investigation did not get underway immediately because of the all-out effort needed to attend to the turmoil at Ground Zero. As the police investigation progressed and they discovered the detailed history of Philip's personal and professional behavior, they no longer felt that she was killed in the Twin Towers collapse. They surmised that she might have been dead even before the attack began.

Lieberman and his wife's family, along with Gallant, however, felt that she was in the vicinity of the attack and when she heard the first plane strike the tower, she rushed to the site to help. Furthermore, Lieberman and Philip's family strongly contested many of the sordid details of her personal life, which the police filed in their report. They alleged that the police did not do a thorough investigation and even fabricated some of their conclusions regarding Philip's behavior. But according to Mark Fass, a reporter working on the case, Lieberman refused to give him access to Gallant's report, "which might have corroborated or refuted the police account" (online article, "Last Seen On September 10th," *New York Magazine*, June 26, 2006).

Litigation Issues

In 2003, after the police investigation ended, Lieberman filed a petition in the New York County Surrogate Court to have his wife declared a casualty of the Twin Tower attacks. The judge, however, turned down the request, stating that it was equally plausible that she could have voluntarily disappeared or might have been murdered.

Later, Philip's name was placed on the list of official victims, but then removed. Lieberman and his wife's family continued to appeal to the courts to have her declared a victim of the attacks. The decisions by the courts and the appeals process by Lieberman and Philip's family went back and forth for a number of years.

After a long court battle, a Manhattan Appeals Court in 2008 held that she died attempting to aid people at Ground Zero. Since payments to all the victims ended in 2003, Lieberman did not receive any money. The average payout the families was $1.8 million. But Sneha Anne Philip's name is recorded on Panel S-66 of the National September 11 Memorial's South Pool. "Sneha Anne Philip," Online article, Wikipedia – the free encyclopedia.)

But what really happened to Philip?

Theories

We'll consider the theories, starting with those we think least likely.

Homicide

What about the possibility that Philip was murdered? Whenever some-one simply disappears, we need to take the possibility of homicide seri-ously. As we have noted, Philip may have been seen on videotape at her apartment the morning of September 11. If this was indeed Philip, the theory that she was caught up in the events at the World Trade Center a short distance away is considerably bolstered. Admittedly, she might have left the lobby, never returning to her apartment after the attacks (remember they did not find her footprints in the dust on the apart-ment floor), gone off somewhere and met her fate at the hands of an unknown person later that day. But we think a murderous attack was more likely to happen the night before than in the turmoil and confu-sion of the day of 9/11.

So let us assume that the woman in the tape is not Sneha. If she were murdered, who killed her? The husband is always the first suspect in disap-pearances of wives. Lieberman and Sneha did have a troubled relationship, her behavior may well have been provoking and we do not know whether Sneha had a life insurance policy. (If so, Lieberman was the likely benefi-ciary). Some Indian families with strict religious traditions who believe in "honor killings" have been known to punish another family member who has sinned or brought disgrace to the family. While it may not be very likely, it is still in the realm of possibility, and as such, we need to mention that Philip might have suffered such a fate.

Sneha was known to frequent gay bars, and apparently, did sometimes go home with a stranger she met there. She might have picked the wrong person and wound up dead at the end of the evening. Finally, she might simply have been the victim of a random attack.

None of these possibilities is especially likely. Although the family yields typical suspects, no evidence at all emerged that either her family or her husband had any violent intent. While going home with strangers is a high-risk behavior, the risk almost always comes from men (either straight or gay) and Sneha did not pick up strange men.

Moreover, in almost all of these options, we would expect that her body would have been found: neither her husband nor her family were the backwoods type who would know of remote hiding places, and muggers and street rapists don't typically hide bodies. It is, of course, possible that she was murdered by an unknown serial killer who did successfully hide the body, but this is a very remote possibility.

There are, perhaps, a few things that might support the murder hypothesis. Most important, Sneha did not spend the night at home: no one has come forward to give an innocent explanation of where she was at the time. Also, as far as we know, the woman Sneha was seen shopping with was never identified, and we might speculate that she played an ominous role and that the items Sneha bought were never recovered. Although these facts could easily fit into a murder scenario, less sinister explanations are readily available. Sneha might well have stayed over with her shopping companion and left the items with her (Or she might have done the same if she had gone home with another woman that she met.). In either case, the woman or women may simply have not wanted to get caught up in the drama and publicity of the case. This might seem especially heartless in the case of the shopping companion who may have been a friend, but it seems more likely than a sudden murder with a successful disposal of a body (especially if theory holds that the killer was a woman).

Suicide

Sneha was facing crises in both her personal and professional lives at the time of her disappearance. Indeed, as we have seen, she had been arraigned on September 10.

But although she might have had a motive, there is no real evidence to support this theory. There are no reports that she made a previous attempt or seemed suicidally depressed. And, again, her body was never found. Although the bodies of some of those who jump off bridges are not recovered, we think that both murder and suicide are about equally implausible. Both are possible, but there are more likely explanations.

Off to a New Life

Let's examine the possibility that Philip chose to disappear. At the beginning of Gallant's investigation, he thought that Philip might have used the attack to flee from her personal problems and start a new life, but then later changed his mind. (In the beginning, Lieberman felt that the police thought that his wife had indeed been killed in the disaster. When they began their investigation, however, the police suspected it was more likely that she had disappeared voluntarily.)

Perhaps this explains why no one came forward to report on her whereabouts on the night of September 10. Philip may have spent it with a confederate (maybe the woman she went shopping with) or have already left. Even if the woman videotaped is Philip, she might have suddenly realized after the attack that the collapse of the Twin Towers gave her a once in a lifetime chance to cover her trail. Philip was a bold woman and could have taken the chance.

This hypothesis does, of course, give a good explanation of why no body was found. But there was nothing on her computer that suggested she was planning to disappear. The fact that she left behind a number of personal items like her glasses, credit cards, passport and driver's license also indicates that she did not vanish purposely. And while Philip was going through problems and did dance to her own drummer, it does not appear that she was so dissatisfied with her life that she wanted to her leave her husband, family and everything else behind.

If she did leave, why has no trace of her been found since? What would she use for money? The only credit card she had was Lieberman's American Express card, which she used for shopping the day before 9/11. There was no further use of the card after that instance. With friends and relatives in India, Philip, unlike many others who disappear, did have a far-off place to go, and if she did get there, could have established a new identity and got lost in the crowd.

This is, we think, more likely than suicide or murder, but is still not supported by any positive evidence.

She Ran to Help

We think it most likely that Philip died in the World Trade Center attacks while attempting to help others. This conclusion seems overwhelmingly likely if the woman on the videotape in their apartment lobby is, in fact, Philip. (Although New York is a huge and diverse city, the resemblance in both appearance – including that her hair and dress were consistent with Philip's image recorded at the Century 21 shopping store – and manner-isms that her husband and family noted are very persuasive. And even if the woman is not Philip, we still think that dying in the attack is the most likely explanation of her disappearance.) In this case, we'll never know why she turned and left without going up her apartment, but she did.

Since the videotaping event in their apartment lobby was near the World Trade Center and occurred shortly before the attack, Philip would quickly have become aware of the disaster. It is reasonable to conclude that when she realized how horrible the incident was, that she would have hastened to the scene to render any assistance to those in need of aid. The first plane hit the North Tower at 8:46 a.m. Eastern time, it collapsed at

10:28 a.m.; the second plane hit the South Tower at 9:03 a.m., it collapsed at 9:59 a.m. Whichever building Philip was in, she may well have spent a considerable time trying to help.

This option makes the best sense of her sudden – and as far as anyone knows – permanent disappearance. While Philips's body was never found at Ground Zero, there are many victims of the attack at the World Trade Center that have not been found.

At the time of the attacks, Philip was most likely wearing her minnu, a traditional Indian wedding pendant with a diamond, which her husband gave her when they got married. While it could have survived the terrific heat at the site, it was never found. Her engagement ring, wedding band and diamond earrings, which she always wore, would also have survived the heat, but they too, were never recovered. These items may be among the artifacts from the site still left unidentified, or they may simply be buried in the earth.

We think she died a hero.

If you have any information about this case, which you feel might be helpful, please call the New York City Police Department at 212-334-0635.

Recommended Reading

Fass, Mark. "Last Seen On September 10th," Online article, *New York Magazine*, June 26, 2006.

"Sneha Anne Phillips," Wikipedia, the free encyclopedia.

Epilogue

Some 13 years after 9/11, forensic scientists using new technology, are still hard at work attempting to match the bone fragments with DNA victims who are still unidentified. From the total of 2,753 who have been reported missing at the trade center, 1,115 victims still have not been identified through DNA. ("Scientists still working to identify 9/11 victims, nearly 13 years later." FOX NEWS, Associated Press, May 9, 2014.)

A Feel Good Story

A small, fragile photo of a wedding group, sitting on the desk in an office on the 77th floor of the second World Trade Center Tower, which was demolished, has astonishingly survived.

It is even more unbelievable, when you consider that the debris from the 9/11 World Trade center disaster has undergone a painstaking identification process. For countless families, nothing has ever been recovered: and sadly never will be. Besides ending 3,000 lives, the terrorist attacks destroyed thousands of records, irreplaceable documents and art: incalculable personal items, valuable jewelry and human bones have also all disappeared.

A young woman who found the wedding photo on the street in New York City amid the rubble of the World Trade Center in 2001 near Ground Zero, gave the picture to Elizabeth Stringer Keefe and told her to do "something meaningful with it." The damaged photo began a 13-year-old search by Elizabeth who wanted to locate the couple in the photo.

The photo, which depicts a bride and groom and two women and two men, was re-tweeted 35,000 times including a colleague of Fred Mahe, who contacted him since Fred was in the photo. Fred, who was working at the World Trade Center in 2001, was getting off the subway just as the attack began, contacted Elizabeth and identified himself as well as the couple in the photo.

Fred, who lives in Colorado, traveled to New York City where he was to see the photo for the first time in 13 years, when he met Elizabeth on Fox News on September 14, 2014. Elizabeth gently and slowly took the photo from a book she was holding and presented it to Fred. He looked and starred at the photo: he clearly was stunned. ("Wedding group in mystery 9/11 photo ID's after woman's Internet hunt." Online article – Fox News September 14, 2014.)

Bonnie and Mitchel: Long Time Gone, Gone

Without a Trace

It's long, long when she's gone
I get weary holding on
Now I'm coldly fading fast
I don't think I'm gonna last, very much longer.

"CHEST FEVER" THE BAND

It was the summer of 1973. The country was captivated watching the Watergate hearings on TV as they witnessed Richard M. Nixon's presidency slowly crumble and tumble right before their eyes. The Arab oil embargo paralyzed the free and open road that American motorists were accustomed to, as they were forced to wait in long gas lines. The blockbuster movie that summer, "The Poseidon Adventure," was the forerunner of other successful movies about titanic ships going down. And two Brooklyn teenagers, Bonnie Bickwit, 15, and Mitchel Weiser 16, were excited as they left Camp Wel-Met in Narrowsburg, New York, on their way to attend a major open air rock concert.

Bonnie and Mitchel were only two out of approximately 600,000 (the numbers vary) young people who headed out to attend a rock festival called Summer Jam in Watkins Glen in upstate New York. The event, which was billed as a follow-up to the Woodstock Music Festival of 1969, featured the highly popular rock groups the Allman Brothers, The Band and The Grateful Dead.

Bonnie and Mitchel, who were both excellent students and classmates in high school, had been dating for over a year. They were confident, independent and not risk averse. They decided to hitchhike from the campsite at Narrowsburg to Watkins Glen, which was about 155 miles to the northwest.

When they left on Friday morning, July 27, they were wearing backpacks and carrying sleeping bags. They were upbeat as they took to the road on their adventurous outing. They were last seen hitchhiking along State Route 97 cheerfully holding up their small sign that read "Watkins Glen."

And then Bonnie and Michel vanished. They were never seen or heard from again.

Background

Bonnie and Mitchel attended John Dewey High School in Brooklyn, a school for gifted, high-achieving students. They were precocious, strong-minded teenagers from stable middle-class Jewish families. They were confident in their ability to make their own decisions, but they were also impatient. Mitchel, in particular, was considered to be dauntless.

Bonnie was only four feet eleven inches and weighed 90 pounds. She had brown hair, and brown eyes. She and Mitchel gave the impression that they were serious about each other. In the summer of 1973, they secretly exchanged wedding rings. During that summer, Bonnie worked at Camp Wel-Met in Narrowsburg about 100 miles north of New York City. Mitchel was employed as a photographer's assistant in Brooklyn.

Family members said that Bonnie and Mitchel seemed on edge and anxious about something before they left for the rock concert in Watkins Glen, but they didn't know what was bothering them. Several days before leaving, Bonnie left Camp Wel-Met without permission went home and took $80 of her savings; her parents were away at the time.

On Friday, July 27, Bonnie asked for the night off from the family she was babysitting at Camp Wel-Met when Mitchel showed up, however, the family refused her request. Bonnie became angry and decided to quit her job. Earlier that day, Mitchel's mom, Shirley, told him that she didn't want him to attend the music festival or to hitchhike there. She also offered him money so he wouldn't have to hitchhike, but she said sadly, "He ran out of the door." Later, she called him at Camp Wel-Met to see if he arrived there safely.

Was something really troubling Bonnie and Mitchel that they kept to themselves? Or was it a case of just two impatient adolescents who wanted to be independent and all grown up too soon?

But, then, whatever happened, they were no more.

Off to the Concert

On July 27, Bonnie and Mitchel had breakfast in the dining room at Camp Wel-Met before they left the campsite and started off for the concert that morning; they had about $100 between them. They were wearing T-shirts, blue jeans and carried backpacks and sleeping bags. They most likely hitchhiked from the campsite to Narrowsburg, which was just a hamlet only five miles away. Scenic State Route 97 was nearby the village, and it was there on that highway that Bonnie and Mitchel were last seen hitchhiking and holding up their small sign that read, "Watkins Glen."

Did They Get There?

There were thousands of people from all directions headed for Watkins Glen that Friday. (If Bonnie and Mitchel made it to the festival, they would have heard the Band perform "Chest Fever.") And, of course, there were many motorists traveling in all types of vehicles on State Route 97 headed to the rock festival.

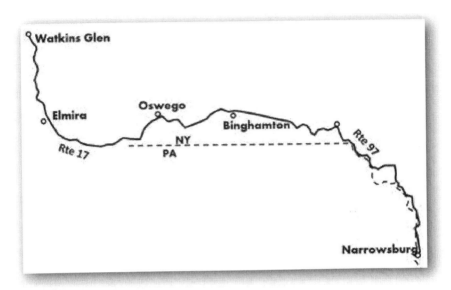

The hitchhiking route Bonnie and Mitchel took—Narrowsburg to Watkins Glen--155 miles.

Hitchhiking was fairly common then and teenagers, especially those headed to a rock concert, didn't mind getting picked up by a stranger. The concert, which was the next day, did not end until just before dawn on Sunday morning. On Monday, July 29, officials at Camp Wel-Met contacted Bonnie's parents telling them that Bonnie had not returned to work.

At first, it appeared to some people that the two teenagers decided to run off together. The families, however, quickly notified the police. The authorities in Sullivan County (where Watkins Glen is located) and the New York City Police felt it was a case of two runaway hippies, which was not terribly uncommon at the time.

The media seemed to drop the story after some initial releases. The grief-stricken families, however, hired a private detective and also sent out thousands of flyers. Relatives pitched in and checked out cult groups and communes, but didn't find any clues as to their whereabouts. The families felt frustrated with the police and even consulted psychics, but that too proved to no avail.

To their classmates and close friends, Bonnie and Mitchel were not radical hippies, but somehow they mysteriously seemed to disappear off the planet. They never contacted anyone, and when the school year started in the fall, they were absent. It was a puzzling case since there was so little information about their disappearance. They were out on the highway hitchhiking and then they suddenly vanished. The families became even more frustrated since the case soon grew cold.

Then one day out of the blue, some years after they disappeared, Mitchel's father Sidney took a collect call from a person who the operator identified as "Bonnie." The caller hung up before the operator was able to connect the call to him. There was never another call and she was never identified. We believe it was someone playing a cruel joke. ("Bickwit, Bonita." Online article, July 27, 1973 -Porchlight International for the Missing & Unidentified.)

The families never gave up in their attempt to find out what happened. They felt from the beginning—rightly in our view--that the police had only conducted a cursory investigation. Then in 1998, 25 years after their disappearance, officials released age-enhanced photos (Bonnie at 40 and Mitchel at 41) nationwide in one more attempt to solve the mystery of what happened. At the time, New York City Police Lt. Philip Mahoney, who was recently appointed commanding officer of the Missing Persons Squad, stated that the files on Bonnie and Mitchel cases could not be located. The authorities in Sullivan County who were the lead investigators in the case, reported that the files on the original case were missing. The families were disappointed and shocked since the dental records of Bonnie and Mitchel were most likely in those missing files. It is unfortunate that the New York Police Department, who were assisting the Sullivan County authorities, did not cooperate more closely from the very beginning. ("Without A TRACE: Without A TRACE," Eric J. Greenberg, Online article, The Jewish Week, July 24, 1998.)

New York's senior sheriff, Michael Maloney, of Schuyler County where Watkins Glen is located, stated that in 1998 the police investigators failed to enter the names of the teens' names in the FBI national data bank, which should have been done. He went on to say that he still recalls Mitchel's father sending him all those flyers 25 years ago.

In 2000, 100 members of the Class of 1975 held a reunion at Dewey High School. They planted an eight-foot red maple tree dedicated to Bonnie and Mitchel. It was not a memorial tribute since there was no evidence that they were dead, but it was the 27th anniversary year of their mystery disappearance.

In the same year, James Horton, deputy chief investigator for the office of the State Attorney General, Eliot Spitzer, was appointed to outline a strategy to take a new look into the Bonnie and Mitchel case. Investigator William Kilgallon from the New York Office of Attorney General and Investigator Roy Streever from the New York State Police, Bureau of Criminal Investigations—Major Crimes, were also assigned to the case. ("State to Move On Missing Teens Case," Online article, Jul 28, 2007,)

The families of Bonnie and Mitchell have never forgotten them. From the time of their disappearance until 2009, Mitchel's family has kept a phone listing in the Brooklyn telephone directory, hoping that Bonnie or Mitchel would call.

And now over 40 years later, Bonnie and Mitchel are still unaccounted for and the unsolved mystery goes on. It's the longest unsolved teen disappearance in the country's history. The families are not only burdened with the loss of their loved ones, but also have to deal with the anxiety of the uncertainty of what happened to them.

Theories

They Just Went Away

Bonnie and Mitchel were loved and came from stable families. There was no domestic violence or anything pathological that would have caused them to run away. Bonnie told her employer, after quitting quit her job, that she would pick up her clothing and paycheck after the concert. At the time, Mitchel was enthusiastic and eager to take his driver's test in several weeks. There was nothing to indicate that they were not planning to return on Sunday. It appears the two strong-minded teenagers were simply thrilled about going to the concert and just wanted to do it with backpacks, bedrolls and hitchhiking. Even if they had run away, emotions would have eventually cooled. Could Mitchel really still be angry 40 years later that his mother wanted him to take the bus? Now in their 50's, would they still fear their families' disapproval of their early marriage? Whether or not they were still together, we find it very hard to believe that they would not have made some contact.

Seeking Medical Care

There is, we think, really only one remotely plausible scenario in which at least one of the two may have survived. Such a scenario would have to take into account the reasons we have just given for thinking that Bonnie or Mitchel, if still living, would at least have let their families know that they were alive. The only such scenario, we think, would be if only one survived and the survivor felt guilty about the other's death. We find it unbelievable that either might have killed the other, but it is just imaginable that Bonnie was pregnant and they went off to seek an abortion with the concert as a pretext. It was reported that they didn't have much money with them, but it's always possible they had secretly saved up some funds. Something went terribly wrong, which resulted in Bonnie's death. Mitchel was so distraught that he decided to run off and start a new life. It is the one scenario that results in one of them still being alive. Of course, getting rid of her body in this scenario would have been a serious problem, and there is no evidence that Bonnie was pregnant. But, unfortunately, we can think of no other scenario that is even remotely likely and leaves at least one of them alive.

A Drowning Fable

In 2000, Alan (other spelling Allyn) Smith, a Navy veteran, told the authorities a strange story. He reported that while he was returning from Watkins Glen after attending the rock concert back in 1973, he managed to get a ride on a Volkswagen bus, which also had Bonnie and Mitchel as passengers.

Since it was a very warm day, the bus driver stopped for a short spell at a river to cool off. Smith said that Bonnie got into difficulty in the water and Mitchel rushed in an attempt to save her, but they both were swept away by the swift river current.

The bus driver told Smith he would report the drowning to the police, but there is no record that the driver reported the accident and the driver was never identified. Smith told the authorities he could not remember the location of the river where the alleged drowning took place. He could not identify Bonnie and Mitchel from photos, and he was unable to describe what they wore. Furthermore, their bodies were never recovered. A perceptive correspondent on Websleuths.com also points out that the whole idea of Bonnie being in the water is odd; she wouldn't swim in jeans and a shirt and was unlikely to take a dip in front of older strangers in her bra and panties.

The police were never able to find anything to corroborate Smith's fanciful story. Some people, however, do make up stories to make themselves feel important or to get attention. Smith only came forward after Bonnie and Mitchel's case received fresh publicity in the media when their classmates drew attention to it on their 27th reunion. If they did die shortly after their disappearance, this would at least be the most consoling scenario—one young lover dies while heroically, but unsuccessfully, trying to save the other. Although possible, it is unsupported by any evidence and Smith's story sounds to us like a happy fiction. ("Bickwit, Bonita." Online article, July 27, 1973, (Porchlight International for the Missing & Unidentified.)

Joy-Seeking Youngsters

Another possibility is that several kids were probably drinking and joy riding about looking for fun. When the oldest youngster in the group, who probably had a handgun, saw Bonnie and Mitchel hitchhiking he ordered the driver to stop and pick them up. After a while, it's likely one of the boys began to molest Bonnie and one thing led to another. Before too long, the driver turned off the main road and went down a small dirt road that led to nowhere. While Mitchel tried to intervene, he was no match for the thugs. Things quickly got out of control and Bonnie and Mitchel were murdered. The panic-stricken youngsters quickly hid the bodies and sped away. This scenario is also not very likely, since the dead bodies would most probably have been discovered.

Malicious Concert Goers

We feel that Bonnie and Mitchel never made it to Watkins Glen. We did, however, look closely at some crowd photos of the concert. One day, one of us, (Chris), pointed out a teenager (up front and to the viewer's right in the photo) that resembled Mitchel. Both our pulses quickened, but we soon realized that it was only a resemblance after all.

It's likely that they got picked up not long after they were on State Road 97, since there would have been many people heading to the concert on that road. Two young men who didn't set out that day to kill anyone may have picked them up. But things began to get out of control. One may have made a pass at Bonnie and Mitchel would have quickly defended her. If the assault on Bonnie was carried out or the struggle with Mitchel became too violent, they may have then proceeded to murder them. After dumping the bodies, the killers were on their way again. Although this is more probable than the other scenarios, there is still the point that the bodies were never found, and killers of this sort would not have been likely to take elaborate means to conceal them. But the countryside around route

97 is often heavily wooded and the killers may simply have gotten lucky. Since so much time has passed, there may be no traces left. But it would be worth seeing whether there are any small roads branching off route 97 and looking for deserted spots along them. The killers would be unlikely to carry out the assault parked on the side of route 97; they were probably not locals and also would have wanted to dispose of the evidence quickly, especially if the killings were unpremeditated. If there are such spots, even now, it may be worth looking for trace of shallow graves.

A Serial Killer

Since the rock festival was a major advertised event, it was only natural that there would be many teenagers hitchhiking their way to the music concert. It was a golden opportunity for a serial killer. He had an unprecedented choice of innocent and gullible victims. He did not have to reside in the area and spend a great deal of time carefully planning out his murder—it was all set up for him.

When the serial killer saw Bonnie and Mitchel, he immediately made his choice. He stopped his van, the teenagers got in quickly and they were on their way. After driving for some time, the killer left the main road and before too long he was parked in an isolated area. The serial killer was cool, ruthless and also skillful at what he did. He may well have found such an area along the road beforehand.

Even though he was dealing with two victims, he had killed before and, no doubt, had thought through the details of his attack. He may simply have restrained them both gaining their compliance with a gun. He then could have carried out the attack nearby or driven them to another, perhaps a more distant area, with which he was familiar. Serial killers often have carefully chosen dumpsites for bodies and such bodies are often never found. And it is the fact that the bodies were never found that makes us think that this scenario is more plausible than the idea just discussed that it was an unplanned killing by one or more people who had not killed before.

In 2001, Mitchel's brother wrote that several inmates in a Maryland jail reported to the police that they overheard a fellow inmate, who was a serial killer, confess to murdering Bonnie and Mitchel. The FBI, who was aware of this serial killer, however, placed him at a different location at the time of the disappearance. Furthermore, detectives who interviewed him considered the psychopath to be unreliable. But even if this person wasn't responsible we think that a serial killer is the most likely possibility.

On that fateful day, Bonnie and Mitchel were in the wrong place. If it had not been them, the thrill-seeking serial killer would have chosen another victim or two on that lonesome highway.

If you have any information about this case, which you feel might be helpful, please call the Sullivan County Sheriff's Department at 914-794-7100.

Recommended Reading

Greenberg, Eric J. "Without A TRACE: Without A TRACE," Online article, The Jewish Week, July 24, 1998.

Glamour Girl Gone

Jean Spangler, a stunning blue-eyed actress, leaves her affluent Wilshire residence in Los Angeles late one Friday afternoon, and walks in a purposefully manner to the Farmers Market just several blocks from her home. She is heading off to confront her ex-husband about an overdue child support payment.

The clerk at the store said that she appeared to be waiting for someone while she browsed around for several hours. At 7:00 p.m., about two hours after leaving her apartment, she called home to ask about her daughter. Shortly afterward, the sultry divorcee just vanished into thin air. She was never seen or heard from again.

It was post World War II, 1949, and Hollywood was booming. The top grossing film was "Samson and Delilah," starring Hedy Lamar and Victor Mature. The best picture of the year was "All the Kings Men" with Broderick Crawford. The two highest paid actors in Hollywood in 1947 were Humphrey Bogart with a yearly salary of $467,361 (equivalent to $5 million in 2014) and Bette Davis who earned $328,000 (equivalent to 3.5 million in 2014).

The average annual salary in the U.S., however, was only $3600; a car cost $1650, and a gallon of gasoline cost 26 cents. NATO was established, Israel was admitted to the United Nations and the Soviet Union detonated its first atomic bomb.

Murder and mayhem were not, however, only occurring in Hollywood films. It was a scary time in Los Angeles. Residents in the city still remembered the "Black Dahlia," the gruesome and much publicized dismemberment of an attractive young aspiring actress, as well as the very recent mysterious disappearance of Mini Boomhower, the Bel-Air socialite who went missing at night with her house lights burning and the front door left wide open. Her purse was found in a telephone booth.

Spangler also went missing at night. Her purse was found with a broken strap two days later in a nearby park. A cryptic note in her handbag led police to investigate suspects that ranged from mobsters to movie stars.

Background

Jean Spangler, the youngest of four children, was born in Seattle, Washington to Martin and Florence Spangler on September 2, 1923. Her family moved frequently, but in 1930 they finally settled in Los Angeles where she attended Franklin High School in Highland Park and graduated in 1941.

Spangler had dark brown hair, sky blue eyes and was seductive. She was cheerful, friendly and well-liked. She was also a vivacious party girl who enjoyed an active social life.

In 1942, shortly after graduating from high school at age 19, she married plastic manufacturer Dexter Benner. Their marriage didn't last very long. She filed for divorce six months later, accusing him of cruelty. They did, however, get back together and in 1944 had a baby daughter named Christine.

When Benner went off to serve in the war, Spangler began a romantic relationship with an Army Air Corps officer known as "Scotty." That extra-marital affair quickly turned bad, and when she left Scotty in 1945 he threatened to kill her.

In 1946 when Spangler and Benner finally got divorced, he was given custody of their child. Spangler then began dancing as a showgirl at Florentine Gardens and the Earl Carroll Theatre, which was known for its glamorous dancing girls. She was also an actress who was known primarily for her small film roles in the 1940s.

For the next two years, Benner refused to let Spangler see her daughter on numerous occasions. Furthermore, he not only threatened Spangler, but also told her to keep away or he would "fix it so she would never see her child again." In 1948, Judge Albert F. Rose awarded Spangler custody of Christine. ("Mystery of Missing Starlet Was Never Solved," Ceilia Rasmussen. Online article, *Los Angeles Times*, October 20, 2002.)

Spangler's life appeared to be going along reasonably well. But on October 7, 1949, which was just another ordinary day, she simply vanished. What happened to the aspiring actress?

A Starlet Goes Missing

Jean Spangler, a 26-year-old divorcee, left her fashionable residence in Los Angeles around 5:00 p.m., leaving her five-year-old daughter Christine with her sister-in-law Sophie. As she kissed her daughter goodbye, she told Sophie that she was going to meet with her ex-husband about an overdue child support payment, and then later go for a night shoot at a Hollywood studio.

As we have seen, Spangler then spent the next two hours apparently waiting for someone at a nearby Farmers Market. About 7:00 p.m., Spangler called her apartment to ask about her daughter and told Sophie that she would return later that night.

When Spangler failed to come home by the following day, Sophie went to the Los Angeles Police Department and reported her missing. While the police took down all the details, they felt that the young actress would probably show up in a day or so. After all, this was Hollywood and it was not unusual for a pretty showgirl to go off for a weekend party or a date, and that she would show up in a day or two.

Two days later, on Sunday, October 9, the police quickly changed their mind when a Griffith Park employee found Spangler's purse near the park's Fern Dell entrance. The straps on one side of the handbag had been torn loose as if it had been pulled from her arm. There was no money in the purse, but the police were curious and puzzled by a note in her handbag with the following message:

"Kirk, Can't wait any longer. Going to see Dr. Scott. It will work best this way while Mother is away,"

The brusque note ended with a comma. It seems as if Spangler was going to write something else, but for some reason decided not to finish her thought. ("Jean Spangler," Wikipedia, the free encyclopedia.)

It was a chilling final message.

Searching for Spangler

After Spangler's purse was found, a team of police and a number of volunteers canvassed the vast Griffith Park, but were unable to find any clues to her disappearance. Robbery was ruled out when investigators learned from Sophie that Spangler did not have any money when she left late that afternoon. (Griffith Park is so called after the repetitively named ostrich farmer Col. Griffith J. Griffith who originally owned the land and served only two years for viciously shooting and grievously wounding his wife, Mary. While Griffith was in jail, his wife prudently obtained a divorce--one condition of which was that Griffith would pay for his son's education at Stanford University. The absurd leniency of Griffith's sentence was based on his alleged 'alcoholic insanity," but it may have had more to do with the fact that he was defended by one of America's greatest criminal defense lawyers ever, the flamboyant Earl Rogers. Among other cases, Rogers defended—and got off--Clarence Darrow on charges of jury tampering, despite the fact that Darrow was obviously guilty. Rogers himself had a severe drinking problem, which led to his death at the age of 52. His well-known journalist daughter, Adela Rogers St. John remembers Rogers in the wonderful book, *Final Verdict*.)

The authorities knew that Spangler had a troubled marriage. It was also a matter of public record that Spangler had a long and bitter custody fight with her former husband over their child. Benner quickly became a person of interest since Spangler told Sophie that she was going to meet him that Friday night. When questioned, Benner told the police that he had not met with his ex-wife that evening, and that he had not seen Spangler for several weeks before she disappeared. Benner's recent wife, Lynn, told police that she was with her husband the night Spangler went missing. Spouses, however, are not the most trustworthy of alibis.

Early on in the investigation, the police thought that Spangler might also have been a victim of the "Black Dahlia Killer," even though some time has passed since Elizabeth Short, another dark-haired movie extra had been viciously murdered and dumped in the Los Angeles' Leimert Park. This theory faded when it became clear that Spangler went missing.

The detectives also thought that there might be a connection to the Los Angeles socialite, Mini Boomhower, who vanished only a month before Spangler disappeared. Boomhower's purse was found in a telephone booth. It turned out that after further investigation, the police were unable to make any connection to Spangler's disappearance. Nevertheless, the fact that only a purse was found in both cases is intriguing. Is this a clue that a single person was responsible for the disappearance of both women or might whoever was responsible for Jean vanishing have planted the purse to suggest a link with Boomhower?

The media quickly picked up on the mysterious names in the note and speculation was rampant. The police soon found out that Spangler's mother, Florence, referred to in the note, was visiting relatives in Kentucky at the time. Meanwhile, the authorities were focusing on trying to identify who "Kirk" and "Dr. Scott" were in the note.

Then, rather surprisingly, even before Deputy Chief Thad Brown of the Los Angeles Police Department could begin to investigate Spangler's last hours closely, he received a startling telephone call from the famous movie star Kirk Douglas. The police were curious about the call, because at the time they were unaware of the identity of "Kirk" mentioned in the note. When word got out about Douglas' unexpected call, the media ran with the story and rumors flew.

When the police questioned the actor, he said that Spangler had a small part in a movie they worked on together at Warner Bros. Studio. He told the police that while he spoke to her briefly one day, he had no personal contact with her and had nothing to do with her disappearance.

About two weeks before Spangler vanished, she was also working at Columbia Studios. She had a small part in "*The Pretty Girl*," starring the actor Robert Cummings. Since the movie was completed only two days before she disappeared, the police also questioned Cummings.

The actor told police that one day she was whistling as she walked by his dressing room. "You sound happy," Cummings said. "I am," Spangler replied. "I have a new romance." "Is it serious?" "Not really, but I'm having the time of my life."

The police wondered if "Kirk" mentioned in the note was her new romance. Later, they learned that her new affair of the heart was someone who seemed to have nothing to do with her disappearance.

The case became more complex and mysterious when some of Spangler's close friends told the police that she was pregnant. Did Spangler lie about meeting with her ex-husband? Was she, in fact, planning on meeting with "Dr. Scott" to have an abortion, which was illegal at the time?

The authorities conducted an exhaustive search for the mysterious "Dr. Scott" throughout the Los Angeles area but could not find any connection to Spangler. When the police visited Sunset Strip bars and nightclubs where Spangler was often seen, they learned that a former medical school student known as "Doc" would perform an abortion for a fee.

Investigators then looked into the extra-marital affair she had with an Air Corps Lieutenant named "Scotty" when her husband was in the army. In that relationship, Scotty was not only abusive to Spangler but also threatened to kill her if she broke off their affair. Spangler's lawyer, however, confirmed that she had no contact with Scotty since 1945.

Spangler had a reputation for being a party girl and enjoying the lively nightlife. She was often seen in the company of men who were celebrities. As a result, she had difficulty balancing her domestic life with her ambition to get that one big break to get a movie role that would make her famous.

In their investigation, detectives found that she had been seen in Palm Springs with Davy Ogul, an associate of the infamous organized crime figure Mickey Cohen, the week before she vanished. Ogul, who was under indictment for conspiracy, also disappeared two days before Spangler went missing. Was it a coincidence that they both vanished about the same time? If Ogul was rubbed out and Jean just happened to be along, mob characters are very good at making bodies disappear. Or, did they just go off together?

About four months later, a U.S. Customs agent in El Paso, Texas reported seeing Ogul with a woman who resembled Spangler in a hotel in that city. Police, however, did not find any supporting evidence that either one was alive or that they had been together. There were other sightings that continued to be reported for some time after that, but none of the leads ever panned out.

Benner was finally granted custody of Christine, but he refused to let Florence see her granddaughter. Florence then proceeded to get a court order, which granted her permission to see Christine. Benner defied the court order and fled the state with his daughter.

Meanwhile, the Los Angeles Police department continued circulating Spangler's photo, but none of the leads led anywhere. Furthermore, a nationwide search did not result in anything either. Spangler's fate today is as murky as that Friday night she disappeared over six decades ago. ("Mystery of Missing Starlet Was Never Solved," Ceilia Rasmussen. Online article, *Los Angeles Times*, October 20, 2002.)

Suspects

Kirk Douglas

When Kirk Douglas made that unexpected phone call to Deputy Chief Brown shortly after Spangler disappeared, it raised many eyebrows. Not long afterward when the word got out, the media had a field day. A Hollywood newspaper headline read: "Kirk Douglas Questioned in Girl Mystery."

It was a major story. He was a famous movie star and Spangler, a statuesque brunette, was waiting for that one big chance that could launch her screen career. It made a titillating storyline, but at the time major studios did damage control and protected their film stars.

When Brown questioned Douglas, he said that he was on vacation in Palm Springs when he heard about Spangler's disappearance on a news report. Actor Douglas, who was the star in *Young Man With a Horn*, told police that he hardly knew her, but that she did have a small part in the film, which was still in progress. He went on to say that he recalled talking to her one day, but never saw her again and never dated her.

Florence told the authorities that her daughter mentioned the name Kirk a number of times when she was working at several different studios, but Florence couldn't recall which one. It's most likely that Spangler was referring to Kirk Douglas, but there was nothing unusual about that, after all he was a famous movie star.

There were some who felt that Douglas' story was "fishy," and that he knew more than he was saying. But, then, that goes with the territory. When Deputy Chief Brown questioned Douglas by telephone, he finally cleared him of any wrongdoing.

We feel that while Douglas' quick response was surprising, he wanted to nip the story in the bud to minimize the rumors and sensationalism that was bound to follow. While it was potentially a juicy story, the evidence indicates that he had nothing to do with Spangler's disappearance.

Dexter Benner

It was known that Spangler did not have a happy marriage. She was divorced only six months later, accusing her husband of cruelty. Later, they reconciled their marriage, and in 1944 they had a daughter named Christine.

Their off-and-on relationship went on for another four years. During that time, Spangler was involved in a romantic relationship with an Air Corps Lieutenant while her husband was in the military. That affair resulted in a long and bitter custody battle over their daughter, in which the court awarded Benner custody of the child. Benner then refused to allow Spangler to see Christine, but when he made explicit threatening remarks to Spangler, the court then awarded custody of the child to her. Benner was furious when Christine was given over to Spangler.

Since Spangler's note said that she was on her way to see her former husband that fateful night, the police were eager to talk to Benner. Was he involved in some manner in Spangler's disappearance to get custody of Christine?

When the police questioned Benner, he said that he did not meet with his ex-wife that evening. Benner added that he had not seen Spangler for weeks prior to the night she vanished. Benner's wife confirmed that she was with her husband at the time that Spangler went missing. (Although a wife's testimony here cannot be considered very reliable.)

When the investigators checked with the motion picture studios, they found that there was no filming going on that night, which contradicted what Spangler said. It appears most likely that Spangler lied when she told Sophie where she was going when she left home. Her deception was clearly a cover story for something else she wanted to do.

The authorities felt that Benner's story was credible. He surely was a heel and a cad, and all too many women who have gone missing after saying they had a meeting with their ex-husbands were murdered by these men. But there is no positive evidence showing that he had something to do with his ex-wife's disappearance. Although he cannot be cleared, there are other suspects who are even more promising.

A Hired Mobster

Detectives on the case quickly discovered that Spangler led a spirited social life. She enjoyed being with, as well as being seen in the company of prominent men, including some with connections to the mob.

It was well known that the notorious gang boss Mickey Cohen and his accomplices frequently vacationed and partied in Palm Springs. Police learned that only days before her disappearance, Spangler was also seen at Palm Springs with David Ogul, one of Cohen's henchmen. At the time, Ogul was under indictment for conspiracy charges.

But then, a strange and surprising thing happened. Ogul disappeared only two days after Spangler vanished. The police wondered if Spangler and Ogul might have fled together since he was under indictment for prosecution.

Several months later, Ogul and Spangler were reported seen by a U.S. Customs agent in El Paso, Texas. Investigators looked into this lead, but were unable to come up with anything. While there were other reported sightings of the couple, there was no supporting evidence that they were alive or even together. We feel it is most unlikely that she would have chosen to leave everything and go off with Ogul.

It's possible that Ogul, who was in a position to be a liability to some mob figure, was eliminated to keep him quiet. Some even felt that Spangler might have been murdered with Ogul. We do not know whether Ogul chose to disappear or was murdered by a hitman. But in either case, the hypothesis that Spangler was with him does not explain the found purse. Mob hitmen are not likely to feel the need for such red herrings. If Spangler chose to disappear with Ogul, why would she leave such a misleading clue whose grim suggestion of violence would only torment her family?

An Abortion Issue

We know that Spangler told Sophie that she was on her way that Friday afternoon to meet her ex-husband and later that she was going to work on a movie set. It appears that Spangler intentionally mislead her sister-in-law about what she intended to do when she left home.

It was most likely a cover story to conceal her urgency to see a mysterious "Dr. Scott" to have an abortion. She obviously did not want her pregnancy to become public knowledge, however, some of her close friends suspected that she was pregnant and told the authorities. Furthermore, Spangler's note was clear about her sensitive situation and what she had planned to do about it. Her reference to things working out better while he mother was away, then also made sense.

But why did she write the note? And why was she carrying it in her purse? When the purse was found, it had a broken strap suggesting that someone might have torn it from her hand making it look like a robbery. But then, why would they leave the note in her purse?

The police proceeded to carry out an exhaustive and thorough search to find "Dr. Scott," but they were unable to so; it's likely, however, that it was a fictitious name. "Dr. Scott" might have been a medical doctor who performed abortions, or someone who was a non-professional who had some experience in such matters.

Spangler was apparently faced with an unplanned pregnancy. Deciding on what to do was not only difficult, but also risky, because at the time, it was illegal to perform abortions. Nevertheless, Spangler would not be deterred from what she wanted to do.

Unfortunately, some desperate women attempted to abort themselves, which often resulted in permanent injury. Others, who were pregnant and wished not to be, went to non-professional persons who often "botched" the pregnancy, which also ended in permanent injury and at times even death. Furthermore, many of these abortions were clandestine appointments, which were performed in shabby apartments or sleazy motel rooms. And, there always was a substantial fee for performing the illegal operation.

When Spangler mentioned Kirk's name to her mother while she was working at several different movie sets, she likely was referring to Kirk Douglas. It's understandable that Spangler would have exaggerated how well she knew the famous movie star. The police, however, were never able to determine the identity either of "Kirk," or "Dr. Scott" that were mentioned in the note.

The "Kirk" that Florence mentioned who came to pick up her daughter on several occasions was likely the "Kirk" named in the note. We do not feel that he was some rich, prominent person who Spangler was attempting to blackmail, and that he murdered her or had someone to do his dirty work. He most likely knew about Spangler's pregnancy and might have helped arrange for her to meet with "Dr. Scott." It's likely he was responsible for Spangler's pregnancy and paid for the abortion.

It was, however, very difficult at that time to find a competent medical doctor who would perform such an operation, even if the doctor was well paid. We conclude that Spangler proceeded with the abortion because she was desperate, and as she said in her note, "Can't wait any longer." But tragically, something went terribly wrong and she died while undergoing an illegal operation. "Kirk" and the abortionist panicked, and somehow they managed to hide her body forever. They left the purse behind in the park to throw suspicion on a random attack or a Black Dahlia-like killer without realizing that Spangle's note was in it.

Recommend Reading

Rasmussen, Ccilia. "Mystery of Missing Starlet Was Never Solved," Online article, *Los Angeles Times*, October 20, 2002.

The Angel of Mercy

Dr. Robert Spencer was a physician in my (Harry) hometown of Ashland, Pennsylvania. He was a highly competent doctor with an eleven-room fully equipped hygienic medical center, and was considered one of the best doctors in the entire region.

While Dr. Spencer had the reputation as an excellent diagnostician, he also had a remarkable sideline. The *Los Angeles Times* reported that he performed approximately 30,000 illegal abortions beginning in the mid 1920s and continuing for the next four decades. He also admitted to this figure in an interview later in his life.

By the early 1930s, his name and his work soon spread throughout the entire region. Then, pregnant women from all over the state came to him. As the news continued to spread about Dr. Spencer in the early 1950s, women were coming not only from surrounding states, but also from all over the country.

Women who came to him for an abortion were treated with respect and also received first-rate care. Furthermore, he charged modest fees and often would not charge anything if a patient didn't have any money.

In December 1956, Mary Davies, a twenty-six-year-old single woman died on the operating table in Dr. Spencer's office while undergoing an abortion. Shortly after starting the abortion procedure, his patient ran into difficulty and despite everything Dr. Spencer tried to do to save her life, he was not successful. He reported the death to the county coroner and also called the district attorney.

The prosecution team felt that they had a strong case against Dr. Spencer. On January 15, 1959, a jury of seven men and five women on their third vote found Dr. Spencer not guilty. The headline on the front page of the *Ashland Daily News* the following day read: "Dr. Spencer Acquitted by Jury on Both Charges." The jury contended that the Commonwealth failed to prove its charges of (a) abortion and (b) death by abortion. The acquittal, especially with respect to (a) is very surprising: was this an instance of jury nullification?

I was quite familiar with the location of Dr. Spencer's office and clinic. When I was just a kid, I would always stare at his office when I walked by, because I had heard about "things that went on" in there. Several years later, however, I would just glance discreetly at his clinic as I walked by.

How was Dr. Spencer able to perform all those illegal abortions? Where were the authorities? Why did he choose to jeopardize his superb medical practice, and spend a major part of his professional life doing what he did? His is an astonishing story. I say much more about his controversial life and career in *Big Mine Run*, Harry M. Bobonich. Bloomington, Indiana: AuthorHouse 2005.

USS DORADO (SS - 248) On Eternal Patrol

Those on Eternal Patrol

Lord God, our power evermore,
Whose arm doth reach the ocean floor,
Dive with our men beneath the sea;
Traverse the depths protectively.
O hear us when we pray, and keep
them safe from peril in the deep.

Verse from the Navy Hymn, "Eternal Father."

DAVID B. MILLER (1965)

It is October 12, 1943, and the United States has been in a world war for almost two years. It was a busy time in the war. The Allies launched a bombing attack on the Japanese airfields and port at Rabaul on New Britain in the Bismarck Archipelago in the South West Pacific Area. The next day Italy declared war on its former Axis partner, Germany, and joined the Allies. The following day, 229 American B-17 Flying Fortresses bombed Schweinfurt, Germany for the second time.

On October 11, the New York Yankees defeated the St. Louis Cardinals--four games to one--in the 40th World Series. The Yankees were the first team to win 10 World Series.

And on a sinister note, Jeffrey R. McDonald was born, but in 1979 McDonald, a United States Army Medical Doctor, was convicted of murdering his pregnant wife, and two daughters in a notorious case. Even monsters, we suppose, were cute babies.

About one week earlier on October 6, the USS Dorado (SS-248) slowly sailed from New London, Connecticut for duty in the Pacific by way of the Panama Canal. Lieutenant Commander Earle Caffrey Schneider is in command with a complement of 77 officers and men. After clearing the local waters, the sleek dark hull of the Dorado begins slipping beneath the waves and before long she is totally submerged.

Schneider, stationed in the control room, is calling out orders regarding course, speed and depth. His operating instructions are to maintain radio silence to prevent being recognized by enemy submarines. At the time, German U-boats are creating havoc all along the Atlantic coastline down to South America.

After traveling southward along the Atlantic Coastline for about a week, the Dorado is now steadfastly maneuvering through the Mona Passage. In the late evening on October 12, the Dorado is now in the Caribbean Sea. She is cautiously passing through waters that are also frequented by German U-boats—then suddenly, something goes terribly wrong.

Later, an Allied convoy sailing through that restricted area reported that there was no contact with the Dorado. Why didn't she respond? What happened?

At the time, the Dorado was headed in a southwesterly direction to the United States Navy base in Panama, with October 14 as a scheduled arrival date. She never made it to the Canal Zone. The USS Dorado was lost on her maiden voyage and the 77 men of the crew were never heard from again.

Background

Earle Caffrey Schneider was born on January 20, 1912, in Beaufort, North Carolina. He decided to join the navy during The Great Depression while living in Los Angeles, California. He graduated from the U.S. Naval Academy in 1933, and later went on to graduate from the Navy's Submarine School in 1937.

Shortly afterward, he was assigned to the USS Pompano (SS-181) until November 1941. He then served on the USS Trigger (SS-237) until March 1943. During that assignment, as the Executive Officer and Navigator, he made four war patrols and earned the Silver Star.

For his next assignment, Schneider was selected as the Commanding Officer for the USS Dorado (SS-248), which was a Gato-class submarine. At the time, he was highly respected and above average in experience and ability in submarine operations. He was considered to be one of the top submarine commanders in the navy. After the Dorado was commissioned and completed its sea trials, proving the crew's readiness, she was ready to be sent out on war patrol.

The sleek Gato-class submarines were strong, fast, well armed and had the ability to patrol for long periods of time. They formed the mainstay of America's submarine fleet in World War II. All of the Gatos (with the exception of the USS Dorado) would eventually fight in the Pacific Theater of Operations.

Gato-class submarines would normally operate at around 200 feet, but often would go to 300 feet. And in emergencies, would dive to 400 feet, though some were even known to go deeper, straining the limits of their hulls to the maximum.

The USS Dorado (SS-248) was one of 52 U.S. submarines that were lost in World War II. Submarine veterans of that war, however, did not think of their comrades as "lost." They rather thought of them in their final resting place beneath the sea and forever on "Eternal Patrol."

Off on Its Maiden Voyage

On October 6, 1943, the Dorado sailed from New London, Connecticut. She was scheduled to proceed down the eastern coast, through the Panama Canal to Pearl Harbor, and then off to join the Pacific Fleet. On October 7, the Dorado was several hundred miles east of Cape May, New Jersey. The following day the Dorado was almost 300 miles east of the Outer Banks of North Carolina. Twenty-four hours later she was about 350 miles off the Bahamas and headed for Mona Passage. (The Mona Passage is a strait that separates the islands of Hispaniola and Puerto Rico; it connects the Atlantic Ocean to the Caribbean Sea.) On October 11, the Dorado reached the entrance to the Mona Passage. And on October 12, she passed through the passage and was in the Caribbean Sea and south of the Dominican Republic. The Dorado traveled silently and confidently, but stayed submerged for the entire voyage. (USS Dorado (SS-248): On Eternal Patrol, by Douglas E. Campbell.)

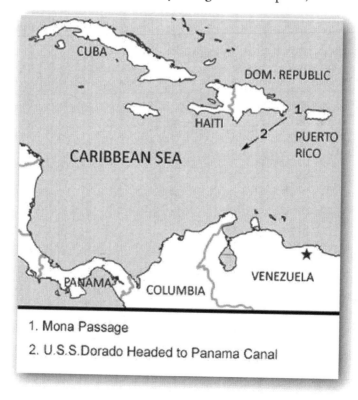

1. Mona Passage

2. U.S.S. Dorado Headed to Panama Canal

The Dorado's Last Day

"Friendly fire" is a surprisingly significant cause of casualties, and this was well recognized in World War II. (On September 10, 1939—just one week after the UK declared war on Germany—the British submarine Triton sank another British sub, HMS Oxley. Only two of Oxley's crew survived.) To avoid such incidents, the normal procedure was to restrict bombing within a 15-mile area on both sides, as well as a 50-mile area ahead and a 100-mile distance astern of an unescorted submarine's course in friendly waters. Such a restriction for the Dorado's passage was sent out to all concerned.

On October 12, a U.S. patrol bomber out of Guantanamo Bay, Cuba, which was to provide air coverage for an Allied convoy that was in the proximity of the Dorado, received incorrect instructions regarding the restricted area. At 8:49 p.m., the patrol plane's aircrew detected what they believed to be an enemy submarine and proceeded to drop three depth charges and one demolition bomb. The demolition bomb and one depth charge were duds. None of the aircrew, however, saw or heard explosions from the other two depth charges. The patrol plane dropped a flare to light up the area, but did not observe any evidence of surface oil or debris.

Was the submarine damaged or sunk in the encounter? If so, was it really a German U-boat or possibly the Dorado?

About two hours later, at 10:49 p.m., the patrol bomber sighted another submarine. When they attempted to communicate with her, the submarine opened fire using its anti-aircraft weapons in response to the plane's recognition signals. The plane circled back to the area, but by then lost sight of the submarine. The chance meeting lasted only several minutes.

Later that evening on October 12, when an Allied convoy passed through the restricted area, they were unable to make contact with the Dorado. When she did not respond, there was more than apprehension and uncertainty about the Dorado, which under normal circumstances should have communicated back to the convoy. Why the silence? Where was she?

The Dorado did not show up on October 14, which was her scheduled date to arrive at the Panama Canal. How could she have vanished on her first voyage out and not even having reached Panama?

Air and surface vessels quickly conducted an extensive search, but they only reported sighting patches of oil and widely scattered debris. The extended broad air and ship search was not successful in locating any wreckage or survivors of the Dorado. *(USS Dorado (SS-248): On Eternal Patrol,* by Douglas E. Campbell.) No sign of her has been found to this day.

Investigation and Inquiry

The U.S. Navy assembled an informal Board of Investigation, which was held at the air squadron's base in Guantanamo, Cuba, shortly after the loss of the Dorado.

The entire aircrew testified in the same manner, namely, that they attacked a German U-boat that was outside the restricted area. The crew described in detail the physical appearance of the enemy submarine, which was decidedly different from a U.S. submarine. As the U-boat was diving beneath the waves, the crew decided to attack and dropped three depth charges and one demolition bomb. After dropping flares to light up the surface of the sea, the crew stated that they only saw a large patch of white water and air bubbles. The board appeared to rely only on the testimony of the aircrew since they were the only eyewitnesses to the bombing.

The Board of Investigation concluded that the patrol plane attacked a German submarine and not the Dorado.

Later, a formal Court of Inquiry at the Washington Navy Yard in Washington, D.C. conducted hearings to determine what happened to the Dorado. The fact-finding Court, which was very thorough, heard testimony from many high-ranking Navy Officers and technical experts. The Court noted the decision of the Board of Investigation in its hearings.

The Court recognized that it was in the aircrew's best interest for all of them to tell the same story. After all, people often cover up their errors in judgment. Furthermore, the crew had sufficient time to discuss among themselves as to what they thought they observed prior to giving testimony.

The Court pointed out that the aircrew did not have any special training in determining the difference between a U.S. submarine and a U-boat. Moreover, the encounter took place at night in actual battle conditions and eyewitnesses have been known to make errors in judgment about whether a target is friendly or not.

Some crew members on several of the Allied convoy vessels stated that they heard explosions, and felt the concussions from depth charges at approximately the same time the patrol bomber dropped its bombs on the submarine. An extensive search of the area of the attack, however, did not detect any survivors or wreckage.

The Court of Inquiry, in its deliberations, had a different view from the Board of Investigation. The court concluded that it was highly likely that the USS Dorado was lost because of the attack by the patrol bomber. It was not known, however, whether the Dorado was sunk shortly after the bombing, or that it was damaged and unable to communicate or operate normally and sank later. The average depth of the Caribbean Sea where the Dorado was attacked was approximately 8,665 feet.

Finally, the Court stated in no uncertain terms that it was the surface plot officer at the Joint Operations Center, Naval Operating Base, Guantanamo, who made a serious course plotting error, and provided the wrong information to the aircraft that was responsible for the loss of the Dorado. ("Subsowespac.org. Pacific War Book Review," Ed. Howard. Online article, Updated March 22, 2013.)

Post War Evidence

An examination of German War Records showed that the first attack by the patrol bomber was not on a German U-boat, but must have been on the Dorado since there were no U-boats in that immediate area at the time.

The German mine-laying U-boat 214, which had observed the flares dropped by the patrol bomber, was curious and cautiously proceeded to the area to investigate what was going on. When the crew of the patrol bomber sighted her, they attempted to communicate with her, but the U-214 quickly opened fire on the plane. The encounter only lasted several minutes when the plane lost sight of the submarine.

The evidence indicates that the Dorado was the target of the patrol bomber and not the U-boat 214. Furthermore, there was no record of an attack by U-214 on any other submarine at the time. ("Subsowespac.org. USS Dorado (SS-248)," Ed Howard. Online article. Updated March 22, 2013.)

U.S. and German Mines

Mines were a major cause of the loss of submarines in WW II. When one examines the Dorado case, it is remarkable how many different mines could have threatened her. It is a stark reminder of how very dangerous submarine service was.

The United States deployed many mines in the waterway leading to the Panama Canal to protect it from enemy intruders. They planted contact mines, which were partially submerged and exploded when a vessel ran into one of them. Other, more complex, mines were laid on the seabed and exploded (due to a difference in water pressure) when a vessel came within a certain distance of one of them. While it might not have been very likely, the Dorado could possibly have been sunk when one of those contact mines broke from where it was originally moored, and floated out into the Caribbean Sea.

The Germans were keenly aware of the large marine traffic sailing through the Mona Passage, into the Caribbean Sea and through the Panama Canal. On October 8, U-214 laid 15 mines near Colon, which was near to the entrance to the Panama Canal. They were not, however, detected by the United States until October 16, when minesweepers began clearing ten of the mines. The others were never found. Is it possible that the Dorado was sunk by one of those mines?

Then on October 13-14, U-214 laid several drifting mines, which floated on the surface and exploded when it came in contact with a ship or submarine. These drifting mines were designed to stay afloat for three days, after that, they automatically sank. They were laid in an area in the Caribbean Sea where the Dorado could have possibly come in contact with one of them.

On October 15, U-214 reported hearing a heavy explosion followed by several others similar to it. No other vessels were lost during this time in the area to account for the explosions. Did those explosions come from the Dorado when it came in contact with one of those mines? ("Subsowespac.org. USS Dorado (SS-248)," Ed Howard. Online article. Updated March 22, 2013.)

Theories

Operational Loss

The Gato-class diesel electric submarines were the backbone of the U.S. Submarine Service in World War II, and they saw extensive duty in the Pacific War.

The USS Dorado (SS-248), a new Gato-class submarine, had recently been commissioned. The Court of Inquiry, which conducted a very thorough investigation, determined that the USS Dorado left port in top condition with a full complement of experienced officers and crew. The Commanding Officer, Earle Caffrey Schneider was considered to be a highly trained and respected submarine officer.

It is, of course, always possible that something on such a complex boat can malfunction and cause an operational loss. The Dorado, however, was only underway six days when it mysteriously disappeared. But the newness of the Dorado cuts both ways: while its equipment would not have worn out, the crew would not have been fully familiar with the Dorado and any potential defects. The life of a submarine is precarious: if it is running at depth and its diving planes jam, it has little time to correct the problem before it is driven too deep. Nevertheless, we think the loss of the Dorado due to operational causalities alone is not the most likely possibility.

An Enemy Submarine

The patrol bomber based at Guantanamo Bay, Cuba, that provided air cover for an Allied convoy did not drop its bombs on an enemy submarine. U-214, which went to investigate the flares dropped by the patrol bomber, was the only U-boat in the immediate vicinity.

There were other U-boats operating in the general area at the time, however, they all returned home safely and none reported that they had attacked another submarine. Furthermore, none of these submarines planted any mines in the area.

The evidence is rock solid that the Dorado's loss due to an enemy submarine is essentially zero.

U.S. Mines

The United States laid down not only many mines, but also several different types of mines in the immediate area leading to the Panama Canal to ward off enemy invaders. The contact mines, which were tethered to a concrete pad and floated beneath the surface, exploded when the hull of a vessel hit one of them.

Some of these contact mines would often breakaway from where they were originally positioned, and float away with the existing current. In doing so, these wayward mines endangered friendly shipping.

These mines, however, were planted near the entrance to the Panama Canal and were several hundred miles from the Dorado. It does not appear very likely that one these mines broke loose and floated all that distance and took down the Dorado.

German Mines Near the Panama Canal

On October 8, the German submarine U-214 planted 15 mines about five miles from Colon, which is nearby the entrance to the Panama Canal. The mines were not discovered until a week later, but then it took U.S. mine-sweepers several more weeks to clear out ten of the mines. The remainder of the enemy mines was never found.

It is always possible that the Dorado struck one of these mines. The Dorado, however, was not in the immediate vicinity where the mines were laid. We conclude, therefore, that it is not likely that she struck one of these mines and sank.

More German Mines

On October 13-14, U-214 laid two drifting mines, which we mentioned earlier. They floated on the surface and exploded when they came in contact with the hull of a vessel. The mines were timed to float for three days, after which they automatically sank to the bottom of the Caribbean Sea. Both mines were planted in the vicinity and direction that the Dorado was headed.

One day later, U-214 reported hearing several heavy explosions. No other ship or submarine was reported lost in the region at the time of the explosions.

Did the Dorado strike one of these mines? More on these mines later.

Friendly Fire

The patrol bomber crew unfortunately received the wrong instructions regarding the restricted bombing area. When they saw what appeared to be an enemy submarine, they proceeded to attack it. The aircrew reported that two of the bombs were duds, but could not see or hear any explosions from the other two depth charges they dropped. Even after dropping several flares, they were unable to detect any debris or oil on the surface. Several seamen on different ships in the Allied Convoy did, however, hear and feel the concussions of explosions about that time.

While the patrol bomber most likely did not sink the Dorado since there was no telltale signs (oil and debris) that a submarine went down, it might have damaged her to the extent that she was unable to communicate the nature of the damage she incurred.

There were many friendly fire incidents during World War II, as there were in other wars. From February 28, 1942 to August 30, 1943 alone, there were 13 friendly fire episodes on U.S submarines. The USS Mackerel (SS-204) had the dubious distinction of being fired upon twice. Fortunately, none of these events resulted in the loss of any submarines. *(USS Dorado (SS-248): On Eternal Patrol,* by Douglas E. Campbell.)

Nor has modern technology solved the friendly fire problem: in the Gulf War, about one-quarter of U.S. combat deaths were due to friendly fire. Indeed, modern technology is a two-edged sword. The means of identifying friendly forces are more sophisticated and reliable than before, so there are fewer instances of friendly fire. But the accuracy of artillery and aircraft fire has dramatically increased—so even a single error has a good chance of producing casualties.

Drifting Mine Dooms Dorado

Since the aircrew in the patrol plane from Guantanamo Bay received faulty instructions, they were unaware that they were in a restricted bombing area and proceeded to attack what they thought was an enemy submarine. Two of the four bombs they dropped were duds. Furthermore, the crew was not able to see or hear any explosions from the two remaining depth charges they dropped.

After the patrol plane released several flares, the plane crew did not see any large patches of oil or scattered debris on the surface of the sea. Several crewmembers of an Allied convoy, however, did hear explosions and felt the concussions about the time the depth charges were dropped from the patrol plane. Since there were no enemy submarines in the area, it's clear the plane attacked and bombed the Dorado. Later the convoy tried to communicate with the Dorado, but did not get any response.

We believe the depth charges did not sink the Dorado, but damaged her so that she was unable to communicate and navigate properly. It is not surprising that the Dorado was damaged since the plane was relatively close to her, and besides the Dorado did not have much time to dive deep.

The U.S. mines, which were planted near the Panama Canal, were too far distant to be a serious threat to the Dorado. Even if several mines inadvertently broke loose, it's not very likely that one of them would have cone in contact with the Dorado.

Likewise, the German mines that were laid in the vicinity of the Panama Canal were not a danger to the Dorado since they also were too far away.

The attack on the Dorado by the patrol bomber took place at:

October 12 – 15 degrees – 31' North, 72 degrees - 37' West

Meanwhile, the damaged Dorado continued drifting south in the direction where several German floating mines had just been planted. Let's examine the coordinates of these mines, which we feel are telling. On October 13, the day after the Dorado was bombed, and also the following day, U 214 laid two German drifting mines at the locations designated:

October 13 -- 14 degrees - 57' North, 73 degrees - 21' West
October 14 -- 14 degrees - 57' North, 71 degrees – 51' West

The proximity of the German mines to the Dorado is significant when you consider that on October 15, U-214 reported hearing a loud explosion followed by several other heavy explosions. No other ship or submarine was reported lost in the region at the time of the explosions. Do you think the Commander of U-214 figured out the most like course of the Dorado when he planted those two drifting mines where he did?

The map clearly shows how vulnerable the USS Dorado was, as it headed straight toward the drifting German mines in its final hour.

1. Mona Passage   4. German Mines
2. U.S.S. Dorado Bombed   5. Drifting German Mines
3. U.S. Mines

And so we conclude that the Dorado struck at least one of the drifting German mines and went down. Seven officers and 70 crewmen all lost their lives on the USS Dorado (SS-248), only six days out on her maiden voyage. Arguably, it is the most tragic "friendly fire" incident in U.S. military history.

> All collapsed, and the great shroud
> Of the sea rolled on as it had
> Five thousand years ago.

Moby Dick, Herman Melville

Recommended Reading

Howard, Ed. "Subsowespac.org. USS Dorado (SS-248)," Online article. Updated March 22, 2013.

Where Did Heinrich Go?

It is April 20, 1945, and Berlin is being bombed by Soviet artillery for the first time. It is also Adolph Hitler's 56th birthday and many high-ranking Nazis, including Gestapo Chief Heinrich Müller, are celebrating his name day in a squalid bunker beneath the Reich Chancellery (the Headquarters of the Greater German Reich).

Even on this day several top Nazis are already fleeing the bunker. It's the beginning of an exodus of the final occupants leaving to escape the rapidly approaching Red Army tanks that have reached the outskirts of Berlin.

By April 25, the Soviets have breached the German defensive ring around Berlin and small breakout groups are still fleeing the air-raid shelter. On April 29, Heinrich Müller, however, remains in the bunker and shortly after midnight on that day Hitler decides to marry Eva Braun. The Russians are only 200 yards from the Chancellery. Some are still breaking out from the bunker and others are committing suicide.

On next day, April 30, Hitler takes a cyanide capsule and then shoots himself, while Eva takes cyanide to poison herself. Joseph Goebbels and his wife poison their six children and then they also commit suicide. The Soviet Union forces capture the Reichstag. And the Dachau concentration camp is liberated as the Allies capture the Bavarian capital of Munich.

The Russians finally capture the Chancellery and enter the bunker early in the morning of May 2. Heinrich Müller wasn't there. Did he—either by his own hand or at the hands of some unknown Soviet soldier—wind up as one of the many anonymous corpses scattered throughout Berlin? Or did he escape into the night and fog and make a getaway?

Müller is, by far, the most important Nazi whose fate is still unknown.

Background

Heinrich Müller was born in Munich on April 28, 1901. During World War I, he served as a pilot on the eastern front and was decorated several times including the prestigious Iron Cross First Class.

After the war, he joined the Bavarian police and became active in forcibly putting down Communist uprisings. He displayed ruthless leadership in everything he did and quickly rose through the ranks of the SS (Protective Squadron).

In 1933 when the Nazis came to power, Reinhard Heydrich, (along with Albert Speer, perhaps the most capable of Hitler's henchmen) head of the Security Service, chose Müller to be a close associate. By 1936 when Heydrich became head of the Gestapo (secret police of Nazi Germany), he chose Müeller as its operations chief.

In 1939, Heydrich, Himmler and Müller conceived and initiated a fake attack on a German radio station, with Hitler's approval to have an excuse to start World War II. (The first casualty of W.W. II was probably Franciszek Honiok. He was a German sympathizer of the Poles, and was murdered and left undressed as a saboteur in the false flag attack on a German radio station at Gleiwitz, on the night of August 31, 1939. Hitler cited these attacks as a *casus belli* and German tanks rolled over the Polish border on September 1.) And in that same year Müller was appointed chief of the Reich Main Security Office (RSHA) or chief of the Gestapo, and served in that powerful position until 1945.

As Gestapo chief, Müller supervised the enforcement of Hitler's savage policies against Jews and other groups. He also played a key role in other criminal affairs the Nazi Party carried out. In addition, he managed the security and espionage and counter-espionage operations. For a decade he controlled a legendarily brutal secret police force.

Following the attempted assassination of Hitler in July 1944, he was charged with the questioning and arrest of all those implicated in the plot. Over 5,000 were arrested and approximately 200 were executed.

It is surprising how little people know about Gestapo Müller. Not many would even know his name, and very few would recognize a picture of him. In *A German Requiem*, author Philip Kerr wrote that there were only two photographs of him known to exist.

Müller had a square-shaped face with a high forehead. His stern looking face was not strikingly revealing, but he did have piercing dark eyes and intense thin lips.

He was not only a workaholic, but was a fanatic regarding his duty to the state—it was his mission in life. Müller was a steadfast believer in a German victory, even toward the end of the war.

Fuhrerbunker

The Fuhrerbunker was an air-raid shelter where Hitler and high-ranking Nazis carried out the final stages of World War II. It was part of a subterranean complex with over thirty rooms, vault-like corridors, and many exits that was constructed more than thirty feet beneath the Reich Chancellery in Berlin, Germany. The quarters were not only confining, but also crowded and oppressive. It was similar to living in a concrete submarine. It did, however, withstand the heavy Allied bombing during World War II.

Hitler took up residence there in January 1945, but Eva Braun did not join him until the middle of April. By that time, air raids and shelling were a frequent occurrence. Hitler's birthday on April 20 was a somber event and not many were singing "Happy Birthday," since doomsday was just around the corner. On his 56th birthday, Hitler left his Fuhrerbunker to decorate a group of Hitler Youth soldiers in Berlin. It was his last trip to the surface.

Later that day, as Hermann Göring and Heinrich Himmler were leaving the bunker, Russian motorized vehicles were moving into the suburbs of Berlin. Then on April 22, Joachim von Ribbentrop, Albert Speer and others also left. Meanwhile, the advancing Russians relentlessly pursued their goal—the bunker and Hitler himself.

After midnight on April 29, Hitler married Eva Braun—it was a surrealistic moment. Shortly afterward Hitler dictated his last will and testament. The Russians were only several hundred yards away. Heinrich Müller was still in the bunker.

On April 30, Hitler took cyanide and also shot himself around 3:30 in the afternoon, while Eva committed suicide by taking cyanide. About two weeks earlier, on April 12, Franklin Delano Roosevelt suddenly died in Warm Springs, Georgia. And on April 28, only two days before Hitler's death, Benito Mussolini, and his mistress Clara Petacci, were executed by Italian partisans as they attempted to flee the country. Three world figures go down in three weeks

On May 1, Hitler's private secretary Martin Bormann made a last minute escape. The next day the Russians entered the bunker and Hitler's unshakable belief that the German Reich would last 1000 years was all over—it only lasted 12 years.

Martin Bormann was also never captured. Rumors that he had escaped persisted until 1998 when DNA testing on a skull found near a Berlin railway track confirmed that it was Bormann's, and also confirmed reports that he was killed by Russian fire while attempting to get away on May 1. Of the elite, this leaves only Gestapo Müller as unaccounted for.

Searching for Müller

Counter Intelligence War Room

As the war was winding down, American and British counterespionage officers formed a special investigative unit (Counter Intelligence War Room) to hunt down Germany's military and police intelligence services that survived the war. Müller, as head of the Gestapo, remained an important Nazi for them to capture.

Toward end of May 1945, the War Room prioritized the various factions they attempted to tract down and interrogate. By the end of June, however, the Allies did not capture any high-ranking Gestapo officials. They did, though, seem to think that Müller stayed in Berlin after the collapse of the Nazi regime.

At the time, Europe was in a state of chaos. Many people who were killed or found dead and never identified were still buried. Reports about the possibility of an important dead Nazi official were often misleading or hearsay. Former Nazis would often get rid of their uniform and identification papers. Unfortunately, DNA and other recent advanced technological methods of identification were still in the future. Furthermore, with limited resources, the task of following up numerous leads was painstakingly slow. By the end of 1945, the Allies search for Müller and other Nazis did not turn up anyone important.

The investigators found that there were all too many people named Heinrich Müller. They even found that there were two Heinrich Müllers who were SS Generals, which turned out to be, to say the least, confusing. While they arrested some Gestapo officials, Müller was not among them.

Walter Schellenberg, chief of RSHA's Foreign Intelligence Branch and Muller's rival, told the OSS in 1945 that Müller has been in radio contact with the Soviets. Other Gestapo officers, however, maintained that Müller would never have conspired with the Soviets.

In 1947, the Allied investigative unit searched the home of Anna Schmid, Müller's wartime mistress, on two different occasions. They did not find anything that indicated that Müller might still be alive.

With the beginning of the Cold War in 1947, the Allies began concentrating on dealing with that challenge and the search for Müller waned. Furthermore, the general consensus was that Müller most likely stayed in Berlin after the war and was dead, but never identified.

West German Investigation

In 1960, when the Israelis captured Adolf Eichmann (one of the major organizers of the Holocaust) he told the Israeli investigators that he was of the opinion the Müller was still alive, but did not provide any other information.

With the capture of Eichmann, the West German officials in charge of prosecuting war criminals renewed their search for Müller. They did not, however, think that Müller was working for the Soviet Union. They proceeded to place Müller's family, relatives and former secretary Barbara Hellmuth under surveillance, since they thought that there was a possibility that Müller was corresponding with them.

They also searched the home of Anna Schmid who told the West German officials that she had not seen Müller since sometime late in April 1945, when he handed her a vial of poison and then vanished.

According to a number of witnesses who were interviewed by the West German police in 1961, Müller was seen on the evening of May 1, 1945, the day after Hitler committed suicide. Several eyewitnesses stated that Müller refused to leave the Chancellery with a small group that night, even though the approaching Russians were very close.

Hitler's pilot Hans Baur recalled Müller saying, "We know the Russian methods exactly. I haven't the faintest intention of being taken prisoner by the Russians." The last time anyone saw Müller he was with his radio specialist Christian A. Scholz. Those last few remaining bodies in the bunker were recovered and identified, but neither Mueller nor Scholz was among them.

The West German authorities followed up on reports that Müller's body had been found and buried shortly after the fall of Berlin. While some of the sources did not appear to be dependable, the investigators had no choice--Mueller was an important Nazi and they could not overlook any possible lead.

One story came from Fritz Leopold, a morgue official who stated that Müller's body and others were moved from RSHA Headquarters in 1945 to another location in West Berlin. After the investigators looked into the matter in more detail, they concluded that Leopold's information was not reliable.

A second account originated from Heinz Pannwitz, a colleague of Mueller who had been taken prisoner by the Soviets and then released to West Germany in 1957. Pannwitz told the German Secret Service that the Soviets said that Müller was dead and that his body was found several blocks from the Chancellery. They also stated that he had been shot in the head and that his identification papers were found on his body.

After investigators checked out Leopold's story, the Müller gravesite in West Berlin was exhumed in September 1963, but Mueller was not one of the three bodies that were recovered from the grave.

The German authorities were not able to verify Pannwitz's story. But why would the Soviets give that information to Pannwitz, even if it were true? One might suspect that the soviets wanted their disinformation to get back to the West.

A third report came from Walter Lueders who had been a member of the German civilian fighters. Lueders told the authorities that in the summer of 1945, he had worked with a burial team that discovered a body in the Reich Chancellery, which had the uniform of a Gestapo-General, and that the body had a significant wound in the back. Lueders maintained that while Gestapo Mueller's identification papers were found on the body, it did not have any decorations or medals.

Lueders said that the body was buried in a mass grave in a Jewish Cemetery in the Soviet Sector. The gravesite, which was in East Berlin in 1961, could not be investigated. Furthermore, no attempt has been made to open the gravesite since the reunification of Germany in 1990. The frustration continued, since the German authorities were unable to verify Lueders story.

In 1958, a strange incident occurred, which only added to the confusion. According to the German Armed Forces Information Office, they returned to Müller's family not only the Gestapo's Chief's papers, some of which Lueders claimed to have found on the body, but also Müller's decorations, which neither Leopold nor Lueders claimed to have found. These items were never checked for authenticity. ("Analysis of the Name File of Heinrich Müller," Timothy Naftali et al. Record Group 263: Records of the Central Intelligence Agency. Online article.)

The CIA Search

In the early 1960s, the CIA also began searching for Müller, which was prompted by Lieutenant Colonel Michal Goleniewski's defection to the West. He was the Deputy Chief of Polish Military Counter Intelligence who operated as an undercover agent for the KGB.

From 1948 -1952, he was an interrogator of captured German officials in Poland. Goleniewski provided information on various Nazi intelligence officials, including Müller. He stated that sometime between 1950 -1952, he heard from his Soviet supervisors that they had captured Müller and transported him to Moscow.

The CIA attempted to track down those who supposedly worked with Müller, but were not successful. Subsequently, nothing official came out of the investigation and the authorities concluded that the story was hearsay.

In June 1961, the CIA learned from another source (supposedly a KGB officer) who stated that he read a report that Müller was captured by the Soviet police shortly after World War II. Much later, the defector wrote for the record that he heard from his superiors that Moscow had recruited Müller and that he actually read portions of Müller's debriefing session.

The CIA, however, apparently relied on the West Germans to continue the search for Müller. While there were various reported sightings of Mueller in places like Cuba and Argentina, nothing developed from these stories. The CIA did not pursue this search with vigor for the remainder of the decade.

Stories, however, continued to circulate that Müller was seen in various countries in Europe before leaving for South America. The CIA seemed to think that some of these stories were deliberately released to mislead Allied intelligence agencies.

By 1970 the CIA's Counter-Intelligence Staff, headed up by the legendary James Jesus Angleton, began hearing reports that the Soviets had in their possession important Nazi files that had disappeared from the German archives after the war.

It is not know whether Müller handed over valuable documents to the Soviets, but he certainly knew they would be interested in having them in their possession. It was, in a way, Müller's last bargaining chip. In any event, the Allies never were able to recover those important files.

The CIA concluded that the Soviet and Czechoslovak intelligence agencies purposely started rumors that Müller found safe passage to the West to counteract the Allies charges that Müller escaped to the Soviets.

While there were indications that Müller worked for the Soviets, there is no definite proof for that hypothesis. Likewise, there were signs that Müller died in Berlin, but there was no proof of that.

In 1991 when the Soviet Union collapsed and the archives were opened, there was no evidence to show that Müller worked for them. But, then, the archives could have been purged before they were made available for review. There's always hope, however, that some day we might find out what happened to Müller from files that are presently secret in the former Soviet Union.

In 2012 an English translation of a 2008 German published biography of Heinrich Himmler by German historian Peter Longerich stated that Müller was with Himmler at Flensburg, Germany on May 11, 1945. Both of them the joined SS officers and the small group fled to Bavaria. Longerich wrote that Himmler and Müller separated from each other at Meinstedt. While the author does not provide a source for this story, it might have originated from an interview with Werner Grothmann who was one of Himmler's adjutants. ("Analysis of the Name File of Heinrich Müller," Timothy Naftali et al. Record Group 263: Records of the Central Intelligence Agency. Online article.)

Müller has been portrayed in various fiction roles in books and films. In Philip Kerr's wonderful book *A German Requiem*, Müller (now Dr. Herman Moltke) has escaped from battered and bombed Berlin and is a spy.

But what really happened to Gestapo Müller?

Theories

Suicide

If Müller felt that his situation was hopeless while he was still in the Chancellery, he could have committed suicide--but his body was not found there. A number of major Nazis did choose that way out. Yet Müller could have created false documents and fake his own suicide.

Since Müller was cunning, he most likely felt there was still a chance for him to get away to a safe haven. When he left the Chancellery, he probably would have discarded his uniform and identification papers, however, he would still have found it difficult to move about in bomb gutted Berlin.

In a way, he would have been in a similar situation to the thousands of homeless wandering about just trying to stay alive. Perhaps he thought that it was too late to get out safely—he was trapped. He now viewed his desperate situation as hopeless and that there was no way to save himself. And since he did not want to be taken prisoner by the Russians, he committed suicide—but his body was never found.

While it is always possible that he could have been buried and not identified, as no doubt many had been during that time, we feel it's not likely that he took his own life during those last chaotic days when the Russians captured Berlin.

Fleeing the Bunker

Since Müller decided to leave the Chancellery at the last minute, it would have been extremely difficult for him to get out of Berlin safely. The city was in turmoil and it was not easy to tell friend from foe. Berlin was a ravaged, war-torn city, and looting and shootings were common occurrences. Moving about at night was even more dangerous —killings were not uncommon.

Even if Müller had some kind of transportation, he most likely would not have gone very far before being stopped, since the Russians knew that many Nazis were fleeing the city. By this time, though, Mueller had to act quickly and get out of Berlin. He could not afford to hide out somewhere, in fear of being captured.

Since it was in his nature to be impatient and to have his own way, he most likely took bad risks to breakout in an attempt to save his life. In doing so, he could have easily been accidentally killed or shot.

In this scenario, it's likely he would have been identified, but not necessarily right away. But, then, since his body was never found, we think this theory is also not very likely.

Escape to Another Country

Sometime before the end of the war, many Nazi officials knew that the war was lost and started to make plans to leave Germany. Those Nazis, including Müller, knew that South America was the safest escape-route out of a shattered Europe.

If Müller had decided to leave Germany earlier, his chances of escaping to another country would have been fairly good. Müller, however, was a Nazi loyalist and he remained in the Chancellery until almost the very end. At this stage in the war, his power and influence was minimal, and any potential friends were no longer in position to help him.

Let's assume, though, that he somehow made it out safely to another country or even to South America and remained secretly hidden for years. It would not have been easy for him to remain undetected for the rest of his life, as well as to not have his identity revealed even after his death.

The Israelis, moreover, were relentless after the war and tracked down war criminals for many years. While many Nazi war criminals did flee to South America and were never caught, the Israelis, over time, were successful in hunting down major war criminals.

We think that Müller, the architect of Nazi terror, never made it to another country since he was never found or identified.

Müller and the Soviets

The Allies certainly would liked to have captured Müller because of his powerful position in the Nazi hierarchy, but the Russians were even more interested in getting their hands on him. Müller clearly had figured out his potential value to his major enemies well before the war's end, even though he was a staunch Nazi loyalist.

He realized that he would have to stand trial if captured by the Allies and would eventually be executed. On the other hand, even though he feared the Russians more, he calculated that he would be able to negotiate a favorable deal with them. Müller gambled that he could trade important Nazi documents and information, which could be very useful to them, for his life. In essence, he would spy for the Russians who clearly knew that he was of no value to them in South America.

Müller, who was cunning and devious, would have planned and worked out this arrangement well ahead of the end of the war. So that even during those last turbulent days in Berlin, he would have been able to carry out his clandestine "safe escape" to the Soviets while the city was cut off from the rest of Germany.

The Soviets, of course, circulated rumors and planted stories that Müller had made his escape to the Allies, while they sheltered the Gestapo war criminal. While there were signs that Müller died in Berlin, we think there were much stronger indications that he worked for the Russians. Müller knew he had a bargaining chip that temporarily saved his life, but—he didn't know how long it would last.

We conclude that Müller made a pact with the Devil and sold out to the Soviets. After he was no longer useful to them, he may well have been quietly eliminated.

Epilogue

In 2013, the fate of Heinrich Müller is still uncertain. But *Bild*, a German newspaper, based on documents found by a historian, stated that he died at the end of the war and was buried in a common grave in a Jewish cemetery in central Berlin. The mass circulation newspaper quoted Johannes Tuchel, head of the Memorial to the German Resistance, as saying, "Müller didn't survive the end of the war. His body was interred in 1945 in the Jewish cemetery in Berlin-Mitte in a mass grave."

"*Bild* also printed a document it said was from the registrar's office in Berlin-Mitte showing Müller was buried in the district's Jewish cemetery." ("Nazi Gestapo chief buried in Jewish cemetery." Online article, October 31, 2013. NewsDaily.)

We want to emphasize, however, that we need to be very cautious about reports concerning Müller's death without scientific evidence.

The Simon Wiesenthal Center's top Nazi hunter, Efraim Zuroff, also sounded a note of caution, stating that only DNA evidence could prove Müller was buried in Berlin. "The Nazis' who wanted to escape very often took measures to create false documents faking their death," he said in a telephone interview from London. "I would be very wary of reports like that without forensic evidence." ("Newly Discovered Heinrich Müller Death Certificate Indicates Nazi Head of Gestapo Died in Berlin (PHOTOS)" David Rising. Online article, October 31, 2013.)

Recommended Reading

Naftali, Timothy et al. "Analysis of the Name File of Heinrich Müller." Record Group 263: Records of the Central Intelligence Agency. Online article.

Did They or Didn't They?

It's June 11, 1962, and John F. Kennedy, the 35th President of the United States, is delivering the commencement speech at Yale University and also receiving an honorary degree. It's the year of the Cuban Missile Crisis—the height of the Cold War—when the United States and Soviet Union brought the world to the brink of a nuclear war.

John Glenn became the first American to orbit the earth. The first African-American student, James Meredith, registers at the University of Mississippi, escorted by Federal Marshals. The first Wal-Mart store opens in Arkansas. Bob Dylan releases his debut *Bob Dylan*. The most popular song at the time is "I Can't Stop Loving You," by Ray Charles and the top movie is "Lawrence of Arabia."

And on June 11, four notorious convicts are locked securely in their cells in Alcatraz prison, sometimes referred to as "America's Devil's Island." The escape-proof prison is located on a lonely island in the middle of San Francisco Bay. It is a forbidding place surrounded by the frigid, choppy waters of the Pacific Ocean. Late that foggy Monday night, those four hardened criminals are carrying out one of the most sensational prison escapes in U.S. history.

The next morning security officials are shocked to discover that John and Clarence Anglin, Frank Morris and Allen West fabricated "dummy heads" to deceive the guards into thinking that they were sleeping peacefully in their cells at bed check the previous night.

After crawling through carved out tunnels from their individual cells to a nearby narrow utility corridor (West is unable to make it out in time), the convicts climb up a 30-foot ventilation shaft, and through an air vent to the prison roof. They hurried across the roof, carrying their escape gear and slid down a 50-foot pipe to the ground. They quickly, but quietly, ran across a short field and climbed over a fence. The three convicts then rushed down a rocky hill to the cold water in the Bay.

Now they're facing an even more formidable barrier—navigating the hazardous waters to reach Angel Island, one and three-quarter miles away. Even accomplished swimmers can't remain in the frigid Bay water for more than an hour. While there were 14 attempts to escape from the "Rock," no one has been able to breakout successfully and live to tell about it.

The three resourceful convicts, however, have a homemade inflatable raft, paddles and life jackets. With a quick glance back over their shoulder at their brutal and unforgiving home, they quickly began to paddle across the choppy, treacherous water on their way to freedom. Three shadowy hunched-over figures slowly disappeared into the foggy night—never to be seen or heard from again.

But—did they make it?

Background

In 1846, the United States seized Alcatraz Island, which is in the middle of San Francisco Bay, from the Republic of Mexico. It wasn't until 1859 that it became a U.S. Army fort, and in 1861 it was converted into a U.S. army prison.

In 1934, during The Great Depression, Alcatraz prison was taken over by the Federal government. It was then remodeled and fitted with the newest "escape-proof" safeguards and soon acquired the reputation as a tough and unforgiving penitentiary.

The Rock was home to some of America's most notorious criminals including Al "Scarface" Capone, Machine Gun Kelly and Alvin "Creepy" Karpis--and on occasion a strange personality like the famous Robert "Birdman" Stroud who was a notorious criminal with a superior intellect.

He spent most of his life in various prisons where he became an excellent ornithologist and author. He lived out the last 17 years of his life at Alcatraz prison.

Four other notorious convicts also made history at Alcatraz prison. John Anglin and his brother Clarence (two of 14 children) were born in the early 1930s in Donalsonville, Georgia, but were reared in Ruskin, Florida. They started committing crimes while in their teens, and before long they both were serving time at Florida State Prison in Raiford from which Clarence managed to escape twice. Later, they both began robbing banks together and eventually were sentenced to Atlanta Penitentiary. After they both made several failed attempts to escape, they were sent to Alcatraz in the early 1960s.

Frank Morris was born in Washington, D.C., in 1926 and spent much of his teen years in foster homes. He was considered to be very bright, however, he was sent to reform school three different times. Later, he served time twice at Louisiana's infamous Angola State Penitentiary (where the great bluesman Leadbelly once served time) and also at Raiford state prison. Morris attempted multiple escapes from both institutions. He had a long criminal history prior to being sent to Alcatraz in 1958.

Allen West was born in New York City in 1929. At the early age of 14, he served time at the Georgia State Farm for Boys and escaped three times. Later, he was sentenced to Georgia State Prison for car theft. After his release from prison, he joined the army in 1948 at age 19. He was, however, court-martialed and sent to the federal prison in Lewisburg, Pennsylvania. He was transferred to the U.S. Penitentiary at Atlanta, Georgia for bad behavior.

He was released from prison in 1951, but then sentenced to Florida State Prison, a harsh chain-gang prison, for grand larceny. He then escaped and went on a crime spree crossing state lines, and was finally apprehended and sent to the Penitentiary at Atlanta for the second time. West was difficult to handle at Atlanta, and at the age of 26 was finally sent to Alcatraz.

The four convicts, interestingly enough, met each other while incarcerated at one time or another at Atlanta Federal Penitentiary. By June 1962, each one had been sent to the Rock, the world's most secure prison. But knowing their penchant for breaking out, it was obvious that they did not intend to stay.

It's Breakout Proof

Sometime during the summer of 1961, Allen West, who was the architect of the plan to escape, was moved from one cell in Alcatraz to an entirely different location. His new cell assignment provided him with a much better opportunity to observe the layout of the prison, and he soon began to think about a strategy to escape. West got together with John Anglin and they began to exchange ideas. After a while, John's brother Clarence, and Frank Morris were also brought into the escape plan.

All four convicts were housed in separate cells but close to each other, which allowed them to communicate and work together more closely. For an entire year, they planned meticulously and worked painstakingly at assembling and preparing everything needed for their escape. They took advantage of the fact that each one worked in a different area in the prison, which enabled them to steal tools, materials and anything they could get their hands on to assure a successful breakout.

What follows is a brief description of the overall escape plan. Each convict would tunnel out through an air vent, which was located in his cell to a utility corridor several feet away. From the corridor, they had to climb up the piping in a 30-foot ventilation shaft and exit out to the roof of the prison carrying all of their escape gear. After scurrying across the prison roof, they had to slide down a 50-foot pipe to the ground. Then they had to run across a short field, climb over a fence to the outside world and down a rocky hill to the Bay. At this point, they faced the most challenging obstacle of all—the treacherous, cold Bay waters.

It was an ingenious well-planned escape, although it seemed widely improbable.

How the Cons Conned the Guards

It was late at night and West could hear all kinds of sounds. The wind butting against the windows, and the ever-present sea gulls cawing as they settled in for the night. Some distance away, a bell buoy rang out and the lamenting foghorns blasted out a long moan and a short subdued tone—BEEEoo, BEEEoo.

Inside the prison, some convicts were sleeping while others were tossing and turning, and there were those that snored and some that talked in their sleep. Then there were those who couldn't sleep at all—and if you listened closely--you could hear them sobbing with their face buried in a pillow.

West, however, was consumed with the idea of thinking up an escape plan as early as the summer of 1961. It wasn't until the fall that the four convicts, though, began to discuss in earnest how they might breakout.

One day in the dining hall as John was eating his soup, he realized that his large soupspoon could be used as a tool if it was converted into a pick-like device. Each cell had an air vent about one foot in height and one and one-half feet wide that was located beneath a small sink. The grille covered air vent led to an unguarded utility corridor that was about three feet away. John thought that it might be possible to tunnel through to the corridor.

He soon began making small holes and carefully digging around the air vent in his cell in late November. The others waited impatiently to hear from John on how well the work was progressing. It was not clear at first that this was a viable way out, since the work went very slowly. He was, however, able to chisel away at the damp-damaged concrete surrounding the air vent, using makeshift tools as well as metal spoons he stole from the dining area. Each night the work area around the grille vent had to be concealed with cardboard and painted over to avoid drawing attention to what he was doing. Just getting rid of the dust and debris posed a problem.

When John was convinced that he would in time be able to tunnel through to the utility corridor, the others slowly began to follow his technique. The tunneling was painstakingly slow even though they improvised an electric drill using the small motor from a vacuum cleaner. They worked on tunneling at night when the convicts were allowed to play their musical instruments, which covered up the digging and drilling noise. And of course the prisoners now played a little louder than usual, but not too loud.

Meanwhile they kept busy preparing other items necessary for their escape. West worked as a painter and had access to paints and brushes. John was assigned to the clothing room and was able to steal all kinds of fabric materials. His brother, Clarence, worked in the barbershop and brought back human hair and other items. Morris worked in the industry shop and was able to steal various small, but useful tools. They also had other convicts procure items for them.

By this time, West was getting very concerned since he felt that too many other convicts were hearing about their plan. He also knew that if some con snitched about their planned escape, it was a pass out for the squealer. And it was common knowledge that all prisons had some who snitched to gain favors.

John finally broke through to the utility corridor (only seven weeks before breakout) on April 25, 1962. Now that they were much closer to an escape, they became more excited and intense. After John made it into the corridor, he was eager to climb up the piping in the 30-foot shaft which led to the roof of the prison. But in order for him to do so, they had to make a fake dummy head to put in his bed since he would be spending a considerable amount of time examining the ventilating fan at the top of the shaft when the other convicts were sleeping.

Meanwhile, Clarence had not tunneled through to the corridor from his cell, so he exchanged cells one day (a risky move) with John so he could also climb to the top of the shaft and examine the ventilating van, which was blocking their exit out to the roof. After examining the area at the top of the shaft, they realized there was considerable work to be done, including removing rivets from the vent cover before they could exit to the roof. They also needed to steal a long rope to haul materials up to the top of the shaft, which would now become a work and storage area.

Clarence finally broke through to the corridor about a week after John, so now they needed to make a second fake dummy head. The cleverly constructed lifelike heads were made from toilet tissue, plaster, soap, flesh-toned paint and human hair. The fake heads left in their bed deceived the night guards at bed check. There were, however, additional checks on prisoners throughout the night, but so far the dummy heads worked.

Clarence told West about the ceiling vent and the screws that held everything together at the top of the shaft--they had to be removed and it would take some time. West convinced the authorities that he needed some blankets to hang around the top of the cell block to do his painting more efficiently. Surprisingly, West was given permission to do so, and he hung the blankets so they encircled the ceiling vent allowing his three comrades to work and carry out their escape plan more easily. It turned out to be an important factor in their escape.

With West coordinating the plan, they built an inflatable raft made from stolen raincoats, which were fastened together with thread and rubber cement. The seams were sewed together and then vulcanized by pressing them against the hot water pipes. It was a technique they learned from an article they read in an issue of *Popular Mechanics* that was available to them. They used the same method to make pontoons for each side of the raft and also constructed plywood paddles to navigate it. The crafty convicts made life jackets from raincoats, which were machine-stitched in the glove shop or clothing room. The jackets had a short stem so that the user could grab the stem with his mouth to inflate it. A small clamp was used as an air plug.

Furthermore, they converted a small accordion-like musical instrument, which inmates were allowed to have, into a device to inflate the raft. Since none of these items could be stored in the cells because the guards could and did make cell checks any time they chose, everything was hauled up and stored in the work area at the top of the shaft.

By May 11, (only one month before breakout) Morris also tunneled through to the corridor. It appears that someone else made the third mask because it was very well done. Since other convicts helped them in various ways, it's likely someone who was artistic made the mask.

Morris was agile, smaller in stature and could handle tools well, so he spent a great deal of time climbing up the shaft to remove the rivets from the cover of the air vent. One day while Morris was working diligently in the cramped area but not making much progress, he got a little careless and dropped a wrench. It tumbled down the 30-foot shaft hitting every pipe along the way. Surely some of the guards would investigate the banging noise and their escape plan would be doomed. Four tough convict held their breath—I wonder if they prayed? Fortunately for them, the noise went unnoticed.

By the middle of May, they agreed to move everything they made for their escape to the top of the shaft. That included life vests, the raft, the air pump, paddles and even the masks. Each night someone would crawl from his cell to the corridor and then climb up the shaft and bring the masks down to be placed in their beds.

At the end of May, they were becoming discouraged since the work on the ceiling vent at the top of the shaft was still progressing slowly. The work area was now even more crowded since they stored all their escape gear there. They also needed to do more work on the raft, which was difficult under those adverse conditions.

Furthermore, prison officials had a sense that something was up. The inmates just seemed to be acting a little strange. The prison had an air of expectancy about it--the place was ominously quiet.

It is now Friday, June 8, four days to breakout. Morris had not been able to saw off all the rivets on the ceiling vent fan, but he was making progress. Sunday was a warm pleasant day and all the cons were out in the yard playing horseshoes, softball and other games. Unbelievably, Clarence was shaking hands with some friends and saying "goodbye."

That Sunday night (the day before breakout) Morris climbed the shaft first and lowered down the masks. Morris then quickly got to work on the rivets. John and Clarence joined him at the top and they finished vulcanizing the seams on the raft.

As Morris was busy working on the vent screws, he noticed that the rectangular raft, which originally was six feet wide and 14-feet long, now was smaller and triangular. When Morris questioned the smaller raft, the Anglin brothers were adamant about the change and they got their way; there was nothing Morris could do. Sometime after midnight, Morris finally removed the last rivets and then filled the holes with soap to give the appearance that the rivets had not been tampered with. It was 4:00 a.m. before they finally completed everything for their escape. They returned to their cells excited and exhausted and tried to get a few hours of sleep. I wonder how well they slept? (Adapted from *Breaking the Rock: The Great Escape from Alcatraz,* by Jolene Babyak.)

The Final Day

The next day, Monday, June 11, was D--Day. Morris told West that everything was all set for their escape. West, however, was not pleased to hear that the design of the raft had been changed.

By 7:30 p.m., all the convicts had been returned to their cells as usual for the night. Several hours later, all three masks were in their beds for the last time. When Clarence went to visit West, he was surprised to learn that he was still unable to tunnel through to the corridor. Clarence then told Morris to see if he could help West. While Morris tried, he found that he was unable to do anything. West, in his frustration, blamed the problem on the Anglins.

Meanwhile, John and Clarence were already on top of the shaft and ready to go out, so Morris quickly joined them. West, unfortunately (or so it seemed at the time), had to be left behind. It was about 10:30 p.m., when they finally removed the large vent hood at the top of the shaft; it was like opening the door of freedom. One could only image how excited they were.

Morris exited to the roof first, but didn't take the time to look around and see the Golden Gate Bridge all lit up. Neither did he notice the seagulls flying and soaring above the prison, or the lighthouse beam circling and lighting up the roof area in short intervals of time.

They grabbed their life jackets, raft and other things and ran across the roof and descended a 50-foot-wall by sliding down a bakery exhaust pipe to the ground. From there, they quickly ran a short distance and climbed over a 14-foot barbed wire fence. After that, they had to jump from a cat-walk down 10 feet to the ground. They scampered down a steep craggy hill, across a roadway, down a rocky slope, and finally they reached the cold, perilous Bay water.

The three convicts reached the shoreline around 11:00 p.m. It was the biggest moment in their lives—they finally made it out. They quickly pumped up the raft, assembled their other gear and got ready to leave the island. It's likely it didn't take them too long, but it probably seemed like an eternity.

Finally, the three men climbed into the raft and set their course for Angel Island about one and three-quarter miles away. While the San Francisco shoreline was one and one-quarter miles away, it was populated with people and police. They chose Angel Island, even though they would encounter swifter currents, since the island was sparsely populated and had no cops. Furthermore, once they got to Angel Island, it wasn't much of a problem to cross the stretch of water (the Raccoon Strait) to Marin County from where they calculated they could get away more easily.

We do know that they were in frigid, hazardous and unchartered waters on their way to freedom that Monday night on June 11, 1962. But, what we don't know is--did they make it? For over 50 years, the enduring mystery continues. (Adapted from *Breaking the Rock: The Great Escape from Alcatraz,* by Jolene Babyak.)

West's Ordeal

Meanwhile, West continued to tunnel his way out, and around 1:50 a.m. he finally broke through to the corridor. He returned to his cell and put his mask in his bed. Then he quickly crawled to the corridor and up to the top of the shaft where he saw his life jacket and the other working items his comrades left behind. He hurriedly got out on the prison roof, and ran over to the roof edge where he saw the pipe that his three comrades used to slide down to the ground.

West realized that it was all over. He was left behind standing on the prison roof all alone staring out into the darkness in the direction where his three comrades went. Did the Anglin brothers plan it that way, since they thought it might be easier for three to escape rather than four?

One can only imagine West's despair and anger—he had been abandoned. After a while, he returned to his cell and tried to sleep. Most likely, he twisted and turned in his cot and only dozed off for brief moments until dawn. When morning came, he knew he would be a person of interest.

They're Gone

When the guards made their morning check at 7:00 a.m., they quickly realized that something was wrong. When they looked more closely, they were shocked to see that the Anglin brothers and Morris were not in their beds, but their dummy heads were.

By 7:15 a.m. that morning, the escape siren sounded alerting everyone at the prison. While officials quickly went about their search methodically, it was, nevertheless, a chaotic scene. After a while, the authorities were able to follow the telltale route of the escaped prisoners. The convicts left a trail of materials, supplies, tools and footprints from their cells to the top of the shaft and down to the water's edge. They also left behind a homemade paddle and West's life jacket. When West was interviewed, he spoke freely. The prison authorities felt that he was consistent and likely described the breakout accurately.

When the FBI heard about the escape, they immediately set out for Alcatraz. The investigators got busy quickly looking over all the files, interviewing convicts, guards and other officials. Agents were also photographing everything they felt might be pertinent to the escape. Furthermore,

FBI offices in many major cities across the country were notified of the breakout.

The U.S. Army, Coast Guard and FBI agents participated in the all-out hunt for the convicts. The search ranged from the prison complex to door-to-door legwork in nearby towns to the broad area of the San Francisco Bay as well as the surrounding area of northern California. If the convicts were out there somewhere—the Feds really wanted them. It was one of the largest manhunts in history, rivaling the famous Lindbergh baby kidnapping in 1932. And, surprisingly, the search continues to this day.

On June 12, a handmade paddle similar to the one discovered on the prison roof was found in the water near Angel Island. Two days later, a plastic bag was found between the Rock and Angel Island containing personal effects of the Anglins'. And on the following day, a homemade life jacket was found floating near the shore several miles north of the Golden Gate Bridge that was similar to the one the convicts left back at the prison. Then a week later, a second life jacket was found in the Bay about 75 yards from Alcatraz. The short stem on the life jacket showed teeth marks and the small clamp was missing. Was the wearer one of the convicts who was attempting to keep the jacket inflated?

When the FBI tested both life jackets, which had to be repaired because of tears or punctures, they discovered that while the jackets lost air slowly after about an hour, the wearer could still keep it inflated by blowing air into the stem. West's life jacket, however, which was found back at the prison, remained inflated for hours. The investigators never found the convicts' raft and did not turn up any other physical evidence that could be connected to their escape.

There were, however, many alleged sightings, guesses, made-up stories and even outright lies that came to the attention of the authorities, but none were credible. Detailed accounts of all these stories are covered in Jolene Babyak's excellent book, *Breaking the Rock: The Great Escape from Alcatraz*.

By July 2, the FBI had completed a thorough investigation with no definite conclusion. The agents report stated that no one had seen or heard from the three convicts since the breakout, and that the trio just seemed to have vanished.

Six weeks after their escape, a seaman aboard the *S.S.Noreffjell,* a Norwegian ship, spotted a floating body on the ocean about 20 miles beyond the Golden Gate Bridge. He reported the sighting to the chief officer, who also saw the body, but they never notified anyone, nor was the body ever recovered.

Several months later, when the ship returned to San Francisco, the seaman reported the incident. When the FBI questioned the two men, they said that the floating body was clothed in messy white pants. Were those dirty white trousers really the faded blue dungarees that convicts wear? And was the body one of the escapees? We'll never know.

Accusations and finger pointing were common as investigators began trying to decide who might be held responsible for the prisoner breakout. After considerable debating and bickering, only two officers received minor suspensions. Surprisingly, no one was faulted or punished for allowing the blankets to be hung around the ceiling vent for about six weeks considering that it was crucial in aiding the convicts to escape. A number of prison officials were transferred to other institutions, and several officers resigned, while some retired.

On February 6, 1963, West was transferred from Alcatraz to McNeil Island, Washington. Over the next six years, he served time in several other state prisons and was finally sentenced to Florida State Prison in 1969 where he fatally knifed an inmate. He became ill in December 1978 and was sent to a hospital where he died later in the month. He was 49 years old.

Three weeks later, on March 31, 1963, an aging escape-proof prison with crumbling concrete and out-of-date plumbing became a financial burden to maintain, and Alcatraz was closed. For over 50 years it was the home of some of the most famous criminals in U.S. history.

In 1964, the FBI concluded that after following up all leads, rumors, and other stories that there was no evidence to indicate that the three convicts escaped successfully from Alcatraz and made it to the mainland.

After 17 years, the FBI in 1979 finally closed the Alcatraz escape case. They concluded that the convicts drowned in the cold, rough water of the Bay while attempting to reach Angel Island. The three convicts were officially declared dead.

In that same year, the film *Escape from Alcatraz* was released with Frank Morris played by Clint Eastwood. The movie, typical of Hollywood, strongly suggested that the three convicts made it to the mainland. Furthermore, the warden in the film found a flower on Angel Island, which was a clue that Morris successfully made it out. Actually, there was no concrete evidence related to the escape that was ever found on the island.

In 1993, some alleged evidence surfaced about the escape on "America's Most Wanted" television show. An independent owner of a boat fleet offered a $1 million reward for information that would lead to the arrest and conviction of the three convicts. The alleged evidence evaporated and after a year the reward was withdrawn with no clues, no arrests and no reward.

The stories about the famous escape, however, continued on. In 2003, a "Mythbusters" program on the Discovery Channel tested the possibility of the escape using a raincoat raft, and concluded that it was plausible for the convicts to successfully make their escape.

The U. S. Marshal's Service took over the manhunt from the FBI in 1978. By 2009, the case was continuing to be investigated by the U.S. Marshals Service. Deputy U.S. Marshal Michael Dyke said, "There's no proof they're dead, so we're not going to quit looking."

As recent as 2011, a program on the National Geographic Channel stated that footprints were discovered on Angel Island leading away from a raft. Furthermore, they reported that a vehicle had been stolen that night, which was contrary to what the FBI reported. And the beat goes on—as you can see we are also writing about it.

In 2014, Frank Morris would be in his 80s, while the Anglin brothers would be in their early 90s, if they were still alive. Their names are almost forgotten now, but their ingenious escape has been a fascinating mystery to this day. While we may never find out what really happened, it is always possible that someone, somewhere may come forth with the answer.

Theories

Amazing Escape to Freedom

In its Golden Age, Alcatraz was the ultimate maximum-security prison. The three convicts, nevertheless, did ingeniously break out and actually left the island. They knew about the turbulent Bay water and swift currents, and so they built a sturdy raft and dependable life jackets.

It was about 11:00 p.m., when they reached the Bay water with more than sufficient time to reach the mainland. They quickly inflated the raft and got everything ready for the crossing to Angel Island. One could argue that the Anglin brothers decided that it was more advantageous to paddle off with three men rather than four in the relatively small raft and left West behind on purpose. And if they were even more devious, they could have dumped Morris at some point if they felt their chances of reaching Angel Island were much better without him.

On the other hand, let's assume that the three convicts worked together paddling their raft to Angel Island. While maneuvering frantically against the strong current was grueling work, they were determined and never gave up. The odds were not in their favor, but after several hours and with more than a little luck, they reached Angel Island totally exhausted.

After pausing for a short time, they crossed over to the far side of the island. Since they were good swimmers, they didn't have much difficulty making it across the relatively calm water in the Raccoon Strait to reach the mainland in Marin County several hours before dawn. Now all they needed was some means of transportation. Stealing a car wasn't a big problem for them, since it was something they had done a number of times. After a while, the three bold and cunning convicts managed to steal a vehicle and headed off well before daylight. They were never seen or heard from again.

Since their bodies were never found, this scenario certainly possible. We think it is more likely, however that they did not.

All They Needed Was a Boat

While the three rugged convicts were determined and had grit, their greatest challenge started when they set off in their raft for Angel Island about one and three-quarter miles away.

Unfortunately, they started out at the most inopportune time, since the water was moving in a westerly direction toward the mile-wide Golden Gate Strait and out into the ocean at a rapid velocity. Experts maintained that the convicts would have had a very difficult time paddling north where they were headed. As a result, it's more likely that on that dark night they would have been drifting and floating with the current in a more westerly direction. It would be analogous to walking north in a wide-open area in the dark against a very strong wind blowing from the east.

Even though it was dark, they knew that they were fighting a strong current, and so they were concerned about their progress and direction. Furthermore, as they attempted to head toward Angel Island, their raft would be constantly bucking against the strong current causing it to bounce up and down and before long it would begin to take on water.

They had no efficient way to bail out the water, and besides it meant there would now be one less person to paddle. After a while, their situation became more precarious since they were losing control of the raft and not only drifting, but also in danger of sinking. At this point, they probably started to panic since they realized they would soon find themselves in the water.

It's likely they donned their life jackets and quickly inflated them, however, their clothing and shoes would have a tendency to weigh them down in the water. In any event, they would have had difficulty in the frigid water trying to swim with their life jackets, while the choppy waters were tossing them about. Under those extreme conditions, they were nevertheless still struggling hard and attempting to reach Angel Island.

After some time, they would have become exhausted and in the dark night also found themselves separated from each other. As they gasped for air, they would at times be taking in water and also starting to go under.

They might have stayed afloat for sometime and even lost consciousness, but eventually they would have drowned—one by one. It was all over; they succumbed to those perilous cold Bay waters, never to be recovered.

If by some remote chance, however, they were able to reach Angel Island, they still would have had formidable problems. They had no water, food, money or transportation. There was, however, no evidence found on land suggesting that they got away.

So we conclude that John Anglin, Clarence Anglin and Frank Morris were swept out under the Golden Gate Bridge, into the wide Pacific Ocean and beneath its waves.

If you have any information about this case, which you feel might be helpful, please call 415-436-7677

Recommended Reading

Babyak, Jolene. *Breaking the Rock: The Great Escape from Alcatraz.* Berkeley, California, Ariel Vamp Press, 2001.

Epilogue

Fifty Years and Counting

Even in 2013, U. S. Marshal Michael Dyke, who took over the Alcatraz case in 2003, continues to get tips every several months. He said that one of the most tantalizing clues involved the Anglin's mother, who for years received flowers from an unknown person, and the rumor that her two sons attended her funeral in 1973 disguised in women's apparel even though a number of FBI agents were there in force.

According to Dyke, a statistical perspective also supports the idea at least one or two of the escapees survived the treacherous Bay crossing, because the bodies of two out of every three people who go missing in the San Francisco Bay are recovered. "We have to operate under the assumption they made it," he said.

Mearl Anglin Taylor, one of the two Anglin sisters said, "Just because they did mischievous stuff growing up, they were not bad boys. They never caused no [sic] problems with the family. They just got out and did the mischievous stuff until it got to the bank robbery and that's when they really got into trouble." The other sister Marie Anglin Widner said, "I always believed they made it and I haven't changed my mind about that." (Escape from Alcatraz: 50 years later, mystery remains," Lisa Leff. Online article, Life on NBCNEWS.com, June 12, 2012.)

Maybe she's right.

But—When Did They Leave?

According to reporter Megan Gannon, recent work carried out by some Dutch hydraulic experts simulated a number of possible routes that three inmates from Alcatraz could have chosen for their escape more than 50 years ago.

> We didn't know exactly when the inmates launched their boats, or their precise starting point, and so we decided to release 50 'boats' every 30 minutes between 20:00 and 04:00 (11 p.m. and 4 a.m.) from a range of possible escape spots at Alcatraz to see where they would end up, Fedor Baart, a hydraulic engineer at the Netherlands-based research institute Deltares, said in a statement. We added a paddling effect to the 'boats,' as we assumed the prisoners would paddle as they got closer to land.

If the three inmates left the island before 11:30 p.m., powerful currents would have swept them out to the ocean, according to Baart and his researchers. But if they left between 11:30 and midnight, it's possible that they could have landed at Horseshoe Bay, just north of the Golden Gate Bridge. Their research also indicated that after the landed, any debris could have drifted to Angel Island where the FBI found a wooden paddle and some personal effects of the inmates.

But did they, after all, leave late and were the only prisoners to ever break the Rock? ("Prisoners of 'ingenious' 1962 Alcatraz escape could have survived," by Megan Gannon. Online article, LiveScience, December17, 2014.)

The *White Bird* Disappears

It's May 8, 1927, and Calvin Coolidge is the 30th President of the United States. The national debt is being paid off and unemployment is 4.6%. The Dow Jones Industrial Average is 164, and before the end of the year it is over 200 for the very first time. Movie fans are watching *The Jazz Singer* starring Al Jolson, "My Blue Heaven" is one of the top songs and many are reading *The Complete Sherlock Holmes*. Babe Ruth is the first baseball player to hit 60 home runs in one season. But few have ever heard of Charles Lindbergh.

On this day, Charles Nungesser, an adventurous French flying ace of World War I fame, is seeking to make history. He is planning to fly non-stop from Paris to New York to win the coveted Orteig Prize of $25,000 (equivalent to $339,501 in 2014). He is keenly aware that other competing flyers are also planning to win the huge money prize and that a number have already failed. Nungesser, however, is a fearless, daredevil pilot and the challenge appeals to him.

Meanwhile, rival flyers are closely checking the weather to see who is preparing for the next flight across the Atlantic. Unfortunately, weather forecasters are not able to accurately predict the weather over vast distances. There are no guarantees since storms are always looming out there somewhere. Nevertheless, after several delays due to inclement weather, Nungesser and ace pilot and navigator, Francois Coli, are preparing to takeoff on their nonstop flight across the Atlantic.

It is 3:00 a.m. on May 8, 1927, and their plane, The *White Bird* (*L'Oseau Blanc*), which is loaded with fuel is gently wheeled out from the hanger at

LeBourget Field in Paris. About 5:00 a.m., they climb into the cockpit and shortly afterward Nungesser calls out "Allons," (Let's go). Several minutes later, he shouts, "Contact," the propeller turns and the engine comes to life.

The *White Bird* lumbers down the runway and barely makes it off the ground. The heavily loaded plane rises slowly and seems to struggle to gain altitude. When the plane reaches a safe height, it flies northwest along the Seine River and to the English Channel. The plane then flies over the southwestern part of England and is last seen over Ireland.

The *White Bird* is now flying west on its 3600-mile journey across the ocean. Nungesser and Coli never reach their destination—their plane vanishes. Their disappearance is one of the great mysteries in aviation history.

Background

Charles Nungesser was born on March 15, 1892, in Paris. While he excelled at sports, he was a poor student. At age 16, his father sent him to visit an uncle in Brazil where he remained for five years. In 1914, when World War I began, he returned to France and joined the cavalry.

Nungesser was a swashbuckling adventurer who was always seeking action, so he transferred to the recently formed air force. He earned his wings in 1915 and only one year later became an ace. The flamboyant, daredevil pilot received numerous decorations for his bravery. He had 45 official air victories at the end of the war. He did not escape unharmed and suffered over 15 wounds and almost 40 injuries due to his undisciplined carefree style of flying.

While he was famous, his postwar career did not go well. In 1923, he married Consuelo Hatmaker, a Manhattan socialite, but then she divorced him three years later citing incompatibility. It was a low point in his life since everything he did appeared to be spiraling downward, but then something got his attention.

In 1919 Raymond Orteig, New York City hotel owner, offered $25,000 for the first pilot to fly nonstop across the Atlantic Ocean from Paris to

New York in either direction. If Nungesser won, and he was assured he would, he would then be wealthy and win back Consuelo and be able to support her in the luxurious life style she was accustomed to.

In the summer of 1919, Captain Jack Alcock and Lt. Teddy Brown, two British airmen, accomplished a remarkable--but little remembered--feat. Pilot Alcock and navigator Brown climbed into the open cockpit of their small Vickers Vimy plane at St. Johns, Newfoundland and headed out over the Atlantic Ocean.

They made the first nonstop transatlantic flight when their plane landed some 16 hours later in a boggy field in Ireland. During the flight, Brown miraculously crawled out onto the wings a number of times and used a small knife to chip away the ice from the engine's air intakes.

"In a classic display of British understatement, Brown later recalled his experiences out on the wing as "startling unpleasant,'" according to Richard Bak, *The Big Jump: Lindbergh and the Great Atlantic Air Race.*

Only six months later, Vickers was killed in a flying accident in France. Brown, however, never flew again. And today, nobody remembers their names or what they did.

Their astonishing achievement is even more incredible when you realize that the Wright brothers first flight took place in December, 1903, less than 16 years earlier. Furthermore, they only got off the ground about ten feet in that first historic flight.

Public interest in transatlantic flight had now been ignited following the historic flight of Alcock and Brown. And furious international completion would soon get started to win the much sought-after Orteig prize.

From September 21, 1926 to May 20, 1927, 16 fliers—ten American, four French, one Russian and one Norwegian—competed for the coveted Orteig Prize, which was still unclaimed according to Joe Jackson, *Atlantic Fever.*

Some famous names who participated in the race to fly the Atlantic were: Clarence Chamberlin (American air racer), Richard Byrd (Artic explorer), Rene Fonck (W.W.I French flying ace), Bert Acosta (record setting American aviator), George Noville (American pioneer in polar and trans-Atlantic aviation), Charles Levine (American millionaire entrepreneur and pilot) and Charles Lindbergh (American aviator).

[History remembers the bizarre flight of Douglas Corrigan who was the first man to fly nonstop from New York to Dublin, Ireland, on July 17, 1938, in the dismal days of the Great Depression. Corrigan got into his Curtiss-Robin monoplane at Floyd Bennett Field in Brooklyn, New York and told the authorities that he was headed back to Long Beach, California. He took off and proceeded west, but then made a 180-degree turn and went east. Approximately 28 hours later, he landed at an airfield in Dublin, Ireland. He told a group of amazed airport workers, "Just got in from New York. Where am I? I intended to fly to California." Corrigan became famous overnight. He also claimed that he did not fly the wrong way on purpose. His new name "Wrong-Way" Corrigan, stayed with him all his life.]

The adventurous and impatient Nungesser, however, was untroubled by the series of catastrophes suffered by his rivals. He wanted to be first and he was eager to go.

Can't Wait to Take Off

Nungesser got together with Francois Coli, a World War I French ace pilot and navigator. They designed and built a plane that could fly nonstop from Paris to New York. The fabric-covered plywood biplane, with its double wings carried a crew of two; Nungesser and Coli would sit side-by-side in an open cockpit on their flight across the Atlantic.

The *White Bird's* flying logo was a black heart-shaped field and inside was a skull and cross bones with two candles and a coffin. Nungesser said that the grim emblem on the fuselage was his good luck charm. (Unfortunately, he didn't seem to be right about this.)

Finally on Sunday, May 8, 1927, he decided that this was the day. Early that morning, after the mechanics got his plane ready, Nungesser and Coli climbed into the cockpit. Around 5:15 a.m., with Nungesser at the controls, he waves at the crowd and the *White Bird* moves slowly down the runway . . .

The Roaring Twenties was not only a period of prosperity, but it was also a time of individual daring and pursuing dreams following the desolation of World War I. One of those dreams that colorful and intrepid pilots of that age had was to be the first to fly nonstop across the Atlantic. It was an international race that attracted the most famous and dauntless aviators of that decade. While there were other well-known French flyers also competing in the race across the Atlantic, Nungesser was the darling and sentimental favorite in the French media.

For Clarence Nungesser, everything in his life depended on fulfilling his dream of winning the Orteig Prize—for himself and for France. He and Coli worked diligently and made some crucial decisions in modifying the *White Bird* for their flight across the Atlantic. Their plane was now equipped with three huge tanks that were filled with approximately 900 gallons of fuel. While they took on some light provisions, they decided not to take a radio, parachutes or a life raft in order to keep the weight to a minimum. Even their landing gear, which weighed about 200 pounds, would be jettisoned shortly after takeoff. They also reinforced the fuselage so the *White Bird* could land at their destination in the New York harbor.

By late April, the mechanics had the plane ready to go, but the weather was bad for about a week. Nungesser and Coli were champing at the bit to get started, but the weather continued to be unfit for flying even for the entire first week in May. Everyone was getting nervous and people were constantly asking Nungesser when he was going to take off. Was the long period of inclement weather an omen?

Fighting the Headwinds

Finally, on Saturday May 7, the weather in Paris was fine for the takeoff, but there was some uncertainty about the atmospheric conditions across the ocean in the Newfoundland area, including the rain and fog over the east coast of the United States. Nungesser and Coli, however, decided that they would leave the next day since it was the best break they had in the weather for a number of weeks. It is interesting to note that in aviation circles it was known that it was about 20% more difficult to fly from Paris to New York, due to the headwinds, than flying in the opposite direction.

By 3:00 a.m. on Sunday, the mechanics gently wheeled the *White Bird* from the hanger. After a while, the two aviators arrived at the airport to a cheering and excited crowd. Nungesser and Coli got dressed in their flying suits and climbed into the cockpit to check out all their instruments.

Around 5:15 a.m., they got their final clearance and all eyes were on Nungesser who was at the controls. He shouted, "Contact," and the engine roared to life. Nungesser waved to the crowd, the mechanics pulled away the chocks, and after several tense moments the *White Bird* began to slowly move down the runway.

The crowd held its breath; it seemed to take forever before the heavily loaded plane left the ground. It rose slowly to 60 feet, then 200 feet and at about 900 feet headed northwest along the Seine River. The *White Bird* leveled off at around 1200 feet and then maintained a cruising speed of about 115 miles per hour on its way to the English Channel.

At about 8:00 a.m., a British submarine officer spotted a plane that matched the description of the *White Bird* as it crossed over the southwestern part of England. Around 10:30 a.m., a clergyman and his son, as well as those aboard a small costal ship, saw the plane as it passed over the southern part of Ireland. The *White Bird* slowly disappeared heading west and was never seen again.

Meanwhile, a large crowd began to gather at around 7:00 a.m. the next day at the southern tip of Manhattan Island in New York City. It was a dreary rainy day and the crowd waited patiently for some news or sign of the *White Bird*. Nungesser's brother, Robert, was also one of the many waiting and looking keenly for the *White Bird* to appear. The hours dragged on, and some grew restless while others began to feel anxious that something went wrong.

By late afternoon, there was a growing suspicion that they had crashed somewhere—but where? And by 6:00 p.m., only a small number still stayed on, but diehards, then, always hold out hope.

About the same time there was a media blitz going on in Paris. *Le Presse*, a popular French newspaper, came out with an early edition reporting that Nungesser and Coli had successfully crossed the Atlantic. The article described their sea landing in the New York harbor with cheers from ships that completely surrounded the *White Bird*.

Le Rappel, another French newspaper, also jumped the gun. They proclaimed the triumph of the two French flyers and their successful flight across the ocean; it was a golden age of French aviation. (Adapted from *Atlantic Fever* by Joe Jackson.)

(It's what newspaper editors sometimes do in order to be the first to report a major story, but at times with embarrassing and disastrous results. In 1948, on the morning after the presidential election, the *Chicago Daily Tribune's* headline read "DEWEY DEFEATS TRUMAN." But in the largest political upset in U.S. history, incumbent President Harry Truman, the Democratic nominee, surprised everyone when he defeated Thomas E. Dewey and won the election for President of the United States.)

Searching for *The White Bird*

A huge search began, which covered the entire area from New York to the Newfoundland region for nine days. A sampling of a number of reported sightings, findings, verbal accounts and other information related to the missing plane shows how difficult it was to get verifiable data.

1 - Anna Kelly, who lived near Harbor Grace, which is a small town on the Avalon Peninsula in the province of Newfoundland, said that

she saw a flying object on May 9 that appeared to fit the description of the *White Bird*.

2 - As many as ten other people also stated that they heard or saw a small plane pass overhead on the morning of May 9 in Newfoundland. About 9:00 a.m., Ebeneezer Peddle and his son, James, who were out in a field, just a short distance past Harbor Grace, saw a white-looking plane flying overhead. Elizabeth Munn heard a plane pass over as she was out tending to her chickens. Sergeant Roberts also heard a plane followed by what sounded like a small explosion. Several lobstermen also reported seeing a white plane flying in a southwesterly direction. The interesting thing about all these reports is that they all seemed to follow a reasonable straight line southwest from Harbor Grace to the Gulf of St. Lawrence and down toward Maine.

3 - In the afternoon on May 9, 1927, fisherman Anson Berry, who was fishing in his canoe on Round Lake in eastern Maine, heard a plane approach from the northeast that sputtered like it had engine trouble. Shortly afterward, he heard what sounded like a crash. It was raining and the weather was threatening to get worse so he did not investigate the matter further.

4 - A bizarre story suggests that about that time the rum boat, *Amistad*, which had bootleg rum on board, was anchored southwest of Newfoundland near the small island of St. Pierre that was a familiar hideout for bootleggers during Prohibition. The crew on the boat suspected that the plane, which was flying overhead was carrying U.S. Treasury agents who were doing surveillance work. The boat crew fired at the plane and then heard an explosion. Fishermen on shore also heard the shooting and loud bang. Did the bootleggers shoot down *The White Bird* by mistake? It would be an ignominious fate for brave adventurers! (During Prohibition, it was difficult for Canada to sell their alcoholic beverages to Americans because of pressure from the United States. The ever-resourceful smugglers, however, discovered the small St. Pierre and Miquelon

Islands just off the southern tip of Newfoundland, which belonged to the French since the middle of the 16ᵗʰ century. Since the islands were outside the jurisdiction of Canada and the U.S., huge quantities of whiskey from Canada and several million bottles of champagne from France were exported to the islands and them smuggled into the United States.)

5 - In 1958, a Maine lobsterman reported that he discovered a large part of white wreckage, which he felt might have been part of Nungesser's plane. The actual wreckage somehow got lost.

6 - The search was extensive involving ground and air personnel from America, Canada as well as hunters and fishermen; however, they never found any signs of life or identifiable wreckage of the ill-fated flight. (From *Atlantic Fever* by Joe Jackson.)

Decre's Hunt for the *L'Oiseau Blanc*

In 2007, Bernard Decre, French aviation enthusiast and expert mariner, became interested in searching for Nungesser's plane after he read a story by novelist Clive Cussler and his research for the lost *White Bird* in Maine. Shortly afterward, Decre became obsessed with searching for the plane.

Decre's budget for 2013 was approximately $200,000; he is, however, supported by the French government and Safran, an aerospace and defense company. He continues to investigate the mystery of what happened to the *White Bird*, which he began in 2007.

The following is a summary of corroborating evidence from Decre's research, which also includes some previous findings by others.

1 - A St. Pierre fisherman's diary showed that on May 9, 1927, he heard what sounded like a plane crash and then someone calling for help. He was unable to locate the alleged crash site due to the fog.

2 - Decre found records, which shows that 13 witnesses have heard or saw a plane heading south along Newfoundland's eastern coast, in

addition to at least four residents from St. Pierre who gave similar accounts. (It appears that there might be some overlap with the number mentioned in the previous search findings.)

3 - Residents of St. Pierre and sailors have reported seeing debris in the general area after the *White Bird* disappeared. Fishermen in the area also have dredged up aircraft wreckage around that time.

4 - In searching the National Archives in Washington, D.C., Decre found a U.S. Coast Guard telegram dated August 18, 1927, which described the wreckage of a white plane that was found several hundred miles off the New York coast. Was this the *White Bird* wreckage that drifted downward from the St. Pierre incident mentioned above when the rum boat, *Amistad,* allegedly shot down what might have been Nungesser's plane thinking it was U.S. Treasury agents? Decre thinks that the Coast Guard recovered the wreckage and that it might be stored in a warehouse somewhere.

5 - Decre pointed out that from photographs of the white wreckage the Maine lobsterman found in 1958, which we mentioned earlier, could have come from *White Bird's* cockpit; however, the actual pieces have been lost.

6 - Over the past six years, Decre has gathered about 30 pieces of corroborating evidence, which he suggests is evidence that the *White Bird* did indeed cross the Atlantic.

Decre's theory is that the *White Bird* was blown off its course by bad weather over Newfoundland. Since Nungesser was running out of fuel, he was forced to attempt a sea landing near the small island of St. Pierre off the southern coast of Newfoundland. There is, however, no concrete physical evidence to prove what happened to the *White Bird*.

Nevertheless, for the past four years the Decre research team has been using sonar and a magnetometer in an attempt to find the plane's engine, since that's the only part of the plane that could have survived. The search is difficult because the ocean is vast and there are many other wrecks, which litter the ocean floor. Decre and his team, however, have not given up. ("Is this where the aviation pioneers who vanished while trying to beat Charles Lindbergh crashed? Frenchman identifies tiny island off the Canadian coast," James Daniel. Online article, MailOnline, June 29, 2013.)

They Almost Got There

At first Nungesser planned to fly from Paris to New York alone. Aviation advisors, however, told him that it would be very difficult to concentrate on piloting and navigating the long flight all by himself. Since Nungesser knew about Francois Coli's excellent navigational skills, he decided to team up with him for their flight across the Atlantic.

Then sometime late in March, Nungesser told Paris reporters that he and the stout one-eyed aviator and navigator Coli (he lost his right eye in a flying accident), would fly the Atlantic together.

For Nungesser it was a trade off; he took on a portly navigator but then had the *White Bird* stripped down—no radio, no life raft, or parachutes—to take on more fuel, since he knew he would be bucking against some headwinds over the Atlantic. Nungesser would also be fighting the odds, but the seasoned aviator was a risk taker and never worried about undertaking a quest when the chances of success were very low.

We now pick up their flight as Nungesser and Coli are passing over southern Ireland. They look down and take note of the last bit of land they will see for some time. With a clear open sky overhead and nothing but the vast ocean below, the two aviators are sitting side-by-side in the open cockpit of their beloved *White Bird* and are closely following the 54th Parallel across the Atlantic. One could only wonder how excited and optimistic they were.

The *White Bird* flew along at a cruising speed of about 115 miles per hour, but that was not fast enough for the impatient Nungesser. They constantly checked their instruments and navigational flight plan throughout the flight. While the daytime flying went well, however, flying all through the night was long and tedious as well as uneventful. After flying for about

20 hours, they must have been glad to see the first signs of daylight even though they were still over water with no land in sight.

Early that morning they began to encounter some bad weather, but they had calculated that they would probably spot land in several hours. Shortly afterward, however, they began to confront headwinds, which caused them to use up more fuel. Furthermore, it's likely that the storm, which was brewing began to blow them off course and that used up additional fuel.

Since their visibility was now decreased due to a light fog, Nungesser descended as low as possible in an attempt to site land and then follow the coastline southwest toward their destination. After a while they were relieved to see their first land since crossing over Ireland; it's likely they saw some small islands (probably St. Pierre and Miquelon), which were close to the southern coast of Newfoundland.

By this time, Nungesser realized that they were running low on fuel and that they would probably not make it all the way to New York. He noticed the choppy ocean waves and started to look for a safe place to make a controlled water landing close to the coastline. Was Nungesser thinking at the time that he should have brought his radio along rather than leaving it behind—it didn't weigh that much. There was no way to send a distress call. (The word Mayday is the emergency procedure word internationally as a distress signal. The call is always given three times in a row "Mayday Mayday Mayday." It derives from the French expression "aidez moi," meaning "help me," but by misuse of British sailors, it became "m'aidez," which was later transformed into the English expression "Mayday.") ("Mayday," Online article, Wikipedia, the free encyclopedia.)

As Nungesser was searching for a place to land in the fog and rain, he probably tried to fly as far toward his destination as possible. It's likely he pushed his luck too far and ran out of fuel. As a result, he was unable to make a safe landing and the *White Bird* crashed into the ocean.

Most likely they were injured, perhaps seriously so, and might have been knocked unconscious or killed outright. If by chance they were alive, they would have been helpless and weighed down quickly in their heavy waterlogged flying suits and drowned. The plywood fabric-covered plane would have broken up and scattered about, while the engine would have shortly sunk to the bottom of the ocean.

We based our conclusion on the large body of supporting evidence (plane sightings, wreckage and sightings from numerous witnesses), that Nungesser and Coli attempted a controlled water landing on their way from the Newfoundland area flying southeast toward Maine on May 9.

We acknowledge, however, that all the research efforts have not resulted in anything definite to prove that Nungesser and Coli actually made it to the coastal region of North America. If the Decre research team finds the *White Bird's* engine, then a major aviation mystery will finally have been solved. (Harry was a salvage diver in the U.S. Army during World War II who has searched for lost airplane engines in the ocean. It is very difficult to locate an engine somewhere on the ocean floor; it could also be partially or fully buried. While the Decre team will be using sonar and a magnetometer, they will still also need a lot of luck to find it.)

The alternate theory that the *White Bird* made it to the Maine and crashed somewhere in the mountains is much less likely.

Our heroes are remembered in various ways. There is a stone monument commemorating Charles Nungesser and Francois Coli's takeoff and Charles Lindberg's landing at LeBourget Field. The inscription reads: "A ceux qui tenterent et celui qui accomplit" (To those who tried and the one who succeeded).

Recommended Reading

Jackson, Joe. *Atlantic Fever.* New York, Picador. Farrar, Straus and Giroux, 2012.

Epilogue

Twelve days after Nungesser and Coli took off from Paris, Charles Lindbergh, the barnstorming American aviator, took off from Roosevelt Field on Long Island and became the first to fly nonstop across the Atlantic--from New York to Paris. Lindbergh arrived at Le Bourget Field the next day and landed close to where Nungesser and Coli actually took off.

A fascinating "what if" question to muse. Suppose Nungesser decided to fly alone, and by adding more fuel had been able to land safely in New York. Then what would Lindbergh have decided to do? Since Nungesser had already won the huge Orteig Prize, it's not likely that Lindbergh would not have attempted to fly from New York to Paris.

Suppose the adventurous Lindbergh then decided to take on an even greater challenge--the vast Pacific. But, then, what if he would have vanished over that expansive ocean? It's likely his name would be all but forgotten today.

A Body Tumbled from the Sky

The Fokker Tri-Motor monoplane's engines are already started as it sits at the Croydon Airport outside of London—waiting for its important passenger. Before too long, an elegant and expensive black limousine arrives with Alfred Loewenstein, one of the richest and most powerful men in the world. The plane, with seven people aboard, moves swiftly down the runway and rises smoothly up and over the English Channel on a routine flight to Brussels.

As the plane climbs higher and higher, now reaching about 4000 feet above the sea, it is only a speck in the sky. But, then, a body tumbles from the plane and plummets down into the white--capped choppy waves of the Channel.

The year was 1928. Herbert Hoover was elected 31st President of the United States and Franklin Delano Roosevelt was elected Governor of the State of New York. Bert Hinkle also took off from the same Croydon airport in England and made history by flying solo from the UK to Australia. Mickey Mouse made his first screen debut in "Steamboat Willie," while the top movie of the year was, "The Passion of Joan of Arc." And the two top songs were Al Jolson's "Sonny Boy," and Paul Robeson's "Ol' Man River."

Loewenstein's private plane did not continue on its planned destination to Brussels after a body tumbled out, but quickly landed on a deserted beach on the Normandy Coast, which happened to be on military territory. When questioned by the military personnel, the crew said that at some point Loewenstein decided to go to the bathroom, which was in a small compartment at the rear of the plane, and then -- he vanished.

Loewenstein's puzzling death was an unbelievable freakish disappearance. How could he have vanished in mid-flight, almost a mile high, in the middle of the sky? Was it an accident? Suicide? Murder? Or was it some unexplained mystery? Surprisingly, we continue to ask the same questions today.

Background

Alfred Loewenstein was born on March 11, 1877 in Brussels, Belgium. He learned the financial business from his father who ended up in bankruptcy due to a series of financial crises in the Brussels Stock Exchange.

After his father's death, Loewenstein, who was 20 years old, was left with a sizeable family debt. He risked all the money he had in a Brazilian Company and the gamble paid off. He continued purchasing companies in South America that were not doing well, and ended up making a huge profit. Continuing his streak, he became a wealthy man prior to World War I.

When the war erupted in 1914, he joined the Belgian armed forces but was forced to take refuge in London with his wife, Madeline, and son Robert when the Germans took over Belgium. He was awarded the rank of Captain in the Quartermaster Corps and placed in charge of military supplies, which included purchasing and selling vast quantities of food. By the end of the war, he was an extremely wealthy man. It is not clear how Loewenstein could become so wealthy in such a short time on just a Captain's salary, but it would require great naiveté to believe it was by legitimate means.

Loewenstein continued to maintain his London residence where he operated an investment business. He constantly looked for new opportunities to make money; it was what he lived for. He joined in a business venture with a Canadian investment house, which turned out to be very profitable. His fortune continued to grow and he soon became one of Europe's most powerful financiers.

Loewenstein was not afraid to throw the dice. Through his Belgian housed company, he went on to make an even larger fortune by providing power facilities to poor countries around the globe. By the mid 1920s, he became one of the most powerful businessmen in the world.

People differ as to whether he was one of the brilliant financial minds of the times or a master of the stock market swindle. He had an uncanny ability to make huge amounts of money and at the same time stay within the law—at least as far as anyone could prove. While he was investigated a number of times, the law never was able to lay a hand on him. He did, however, clearly make some enemies in his business dealings.

In 1926, Loewenstein launched "International Holdings and Investments Limited" that brought in large amounts of money from big investors hoping to profit from his known record of successes. The last two years of his life, however, were stressful times since he began to encounter serious business problems with rivals in the corporate world. He also had huge financial reversals and his assets decreased significantly. While Loewenstein was not broke by any means, he was not the money king he once was.

Was his death connected in some way to those recent chaotic years? (*The Man Who Fell From the Sky*, William Norris.)

The Fateful Flight

Just three weeks before his death, Loewenstein's shares in every company he was associated with had been declining slowly in price for several days, but then suddenly their value began to fall hard and fast. It was estimated that his personal wealth decreased by about $31 million (equivalent to about $428.4 million in 2014). Furthermore, he was involved in a long legal battle with Henri Dreyfus, his rival, which was potentially damaging to him.

Nevertheless, with all that was going on in his life, Loewenstein was looking forward to flying home and to his headquarters in Brussels. On July 4, 1928, his Fokker Tri-Motor plane was ready for takeoff. There were a total of seven people on board, including Loewenstein, the pilot Donald Drew and Robert Little, co-pilot and mechanic. His four traveling companions were Fred Baxter, his valet, Arthur Hodgson, his secretary and two stenographers, Eileen Clarke and Paula Bidalon.

It was an excellent day for flying and the plane quickly climbed to 4000 feet and then continued cruising at about 125 miles per hour. Somewhere over the English Channel Loewenstein got up, took of his collar and tie and went to the bathroom, which was in a small compartment at the rear of the plane.

After opening the windowless door to the small compartment, Loewenstein turned to his left, opened the bathroom door and went in. There was also another door (with a small window) on his right as he entered the compartment, which was the exit door from the plane. The bathroom door and the exit door were opposite to each other and only several feet apart.

About ten minutes later, Loewenstein still had not returned. After Baxter and Hodgson had a brief conversation, Baxter decided to check on Loewenstein to see if he was all right. When he went in search of him, he found the bathroom empty. He quickly went forward to the cockpit area and handed the pilot a note stating that Loewenstein was missing. It was strange that Baxter did not say anything about the exit door.

For some unknown reason, the pilot then proceeded to land on a deserted beach near Dunkirk--which turned out to be military territory-- rather than landing at the nearby airfield at St. Inglevert. When the military authorities arrived, the crew told them that they had lost their boss, but then after a while they explained that their employer was, in fact, Alfred Loewenstein. The authorities then instructed the pilot to fly to the St. Inglevert airstrip where the crew repeated their story that Loewenstein went missing.

Unofficial Inquiry

After Loewenstein's wife, Madeline, was notified that her husband was missing, the authorities began a search for his body. Meanwhile,

Madeline requested an informal inquiry for July 9 in order to obtain a death certificate.

Madeline Misonne, who was from a socially well-known family, married Alfred Lowenstein in 1908. Their only son, Robert, was 18 when his father vanished. It appeared that Madeline and her husband had a marriage of convenience. He was totally obsessed with his business ventures and his love of horses. She seemed to enjoy her life of luxurious living, which she had been accustomed to as a young single woman.

The hasty unofficial inquiry was brief, and amazingly no one was asked to give evidence under oath. It was basically a repeat of what the crew had already stated earlier. Judge de la Ruwiere did not grant a death certificate since Loewenstein's body had not been recovered. Drew and Little, however, made a provocative comment. They stated that on their flight back to London that they had conducted an experiment when their plane was traveling at cruising speed and found that the exit door opened easily. The judge concluded that Loewenstein was in the plane just prior to his disappearance and that his death was probably accidental. (*The Man Who Fell From the Sky*, William Norris.)

Why was there no formal inquiry?

Private Autopsy

On July 19, the skipper of a fishing vessel found Loewenstein's body floating face downward in the Channel. He was only wearing silk underwear, silk socks and his shoes. When news of Loewenstein's death was released, the publicly traded shares in all his corporations decreased by more than 50%.

Madeline quickly requested that a private autopsy be performed. The prolonged autopsy, however, wasn't released until September 10. There was no trace of poison and the amount of alcohol in his body was normal. The physicians concluded that his death was the result of falling from such a great height and slamming into the Channel waters. It was strange that the physicians reported that a normal amount of alcohol was found in his body when Loewenstein did not drink or smoke.

The doctors stated that there was no evidence that Loewenstein took his own life and that his death was accidental. They also reported that there was no indication of violence connected to his death. Finally, they said that Loewenstein was still alive when he hit the water. (*The Man Who Fell From the Sky*, William Norris.)

But why was there no official autopsy?

Lowenstein's Bizarre Demise

Immense wealth is often accompanied by conspiracy, mystery and even foul play. Since all that (maybe even the third) was part of Loewenstein's life, was it also somehow connected to his death? While it may be an overstatement to say that the list of people who wanted him dead was the size of a dictionary, he wasn't the most beloved man on the planet.

Loewenstein's death was weird in many ways, but not just because of the manner of how he died. The hasty inquiry where no one was placed under oath was suspect. Even the decision by the judge who concluded that Loewenstein's death was probably accidental was puzzling.

The private autopsy was also controvertible. In essence, there was no fact-finding probe carried out. Was there some powerful outside party involved in the inquiry of his death? In any event, the investigation of his death seemed to end so very quickly and quietly—even though the case made international headlines.

It seems reasonable to assume that all six people on the plane had to know what happened to Loewenstein. They were there—and they were all guilty to some extent. But that does not mean they were the only guilty party.

There was, however, no piece of incontrovertible, incriminating evidence that led to any one suspect. There were, though, rumors, allegations, speculations and some theories as to how and why Loewenstein's life ended so curiously.

Theories

D. B. Cooperesque

Some suggested that Loewenstein might have parachuted out of the plane and was then picked up by a waiting yacht. And of course, speedily carried off to a secret destination in order to avoid facing the collapse of his once fabulous empire.

It should be pointed out that a French fisherman remembered seeing something similar to a parachute falling out of the sky about the time Loewenstein disappeared. Was it Loewenstein's body, the exit door or something else? The rear door of the plane was never found. (More below on the idea that there was a fake door.)

We don't think that this was not an early model for D. B. Cooper, but fanciful suggestion has some charm.

Spouse Betrayal

Madeline was accustomed to living a luxurious life. She was always lavishly dressed and adorned with expensive jewelry. She also had mansions in three different countries in Europe with a full housekeeping staff in each one.

While the Loewensteins were a strange couple with completely different interests, that did not seem to be a conflict in their marriage. He devoted all his time to making money and she was happy spending it.

There was speculation by some that since Loewenstein's fortune had dwindled drastically over the last few weeks of his life, that Madeline feared the family fortune would soon end. Did she conspire with Drew, who was a womanizer and enjoyed the good life, to do away with her husband so that she could maintain her lavish way of living? And also could it be that Madeline, who was much younger than her husband, was romantically involved with Drew?

Since their marriage was one of convenience; it is understandable that there would be some speculation and suspicion that this scenario was a possibility. We feel, however, that Madeline was satisfied with her married life and that there was nothing to indicate that she would be party to arrangement to murder her husband. So we conclude that while this scenario is possible, it is not very likely all.

Accidental Death

Drew and Little rather quickly went on record stating that it was fairly easy to open the exit door on the plane while it was in normal flight. At the preliminary hearing, Judge de la Runwiere based his decision on that information and concluded that the accident theory was plausible. Later experiments, however, showed that one man would not have been able to open the door all by himself (at least not without an extraordinary effort that would rule out an accident).

If Loewenstein became confused when he left the bathroom and inadvertently attempted to open the exit door, he would not have been able to so. He would have simply approached the door and tried to open it in a normal manner like he would open any door. Also, the door was clearly marked "EXIT."

We feel the accident theory is not plausible.

The Fake Door

Author William Norris proposed a theory whereby the killers removed the original door from the plane beforehand and replaced it with a fake door.

The original door was stored in the rear compartment of the plane. The fake door was then installed in such a manner that it could easily be removed rather than trying to force it open against the slipstream while in flight.

As they had planned, the killers removed the fake door while flying over the Channel and tossed it out and then also quickly shoved Loewenstein out. When Drew landed on the beach, they rushed to install the original door back in place before the military authorities arrived.

While this theory is possible, it is complex and would have been very difficult to carry out. Just getting a fake door made could be a problem, since the manufacturer might have contacted the authorities when Loewenstein's death became public. Furthermore, removing the original door, storing it and replacing it with the false door had to be done in secret. Landing on the beach without a door was also risky. What if the authorities were at the beach site when they landed, or had shown up before the crew had a chance to remove the original door from the storage compartment and install it back in its normal place on the plane?

Complexity tends to involve more risk-taking. This scenario begs the question—why choose such a complex way to murder such a high profile person?

Suicide

Just several weeks before his death, the publicly traded shares in all Loewenstein's companies dropped drastically and this was obviously of great concern to him. Did he assume that his corporate empire was on the verge of collapse? Some speculated that corrupt business dealings connected to him were about to be exposed, and that also was a matter of worry and anxiety to him. Was he so distraught that he chose to take his own life?

When Loewenstein got up out of his seat, he took off his collar and tie before leaving the main cabin to go to the bathroom. When he opened the door to the small compartment, he turned to his right and toward the exit door. In this frame of mind, he was determined to open the door. It's also likely that he was quite familiar with how the door operated.

Since Loewenstein was stockily built and rather strong, it's possible that a sturdy man with grit and determination could have opened the door slightly at first. Then, by jamming his foot into the door opening, he could have turned to one side and forced himself out.

Contrast Loewensteins's hell-bent determination to get out at all costs with those who carried out various experiments earlier but were held with safety lines. The experimenters concluded that while one strong person might be able to open the door slightly, he could not force himself out entirely.

The forces that prevented Loewenstein from accidentally opening the exit door did not prevail; in this case, Loewenstein overcame those forces with sheer will power.

The argument that the open exit door would have caused an air blast felt in the main cabin alerting the crew that something happened, which they needed to investigate is somewhat debatable. Loewenstein would have simply closed the door to the main cabin as he entered the small compartment. If so, it is hard to say how far a pressure drop might have been noticed in the cabin if the door were opened briefly. the conspiracy group of six on the plane would have said whatever served their purpose.

We conclude that suicide was a possibility.

Valet Treachery

Baxter and Hodgson were not just employees; they seemed to have a very good working relationship with Loewenstein. Baxter, who was his valet, traveled with Loewenstein wherever he went. Hodgson, on the other hand, was his secretary and also a very close confidant.

It was Baxter, after talking with Hodgson for a minute, who went to the bathroom to check on Loewenstein when he did not return to the main cabin. Did they both harbor some secret grudge against their boss that would cause them to push him out of the plane? Why did they state that Loewenstein had been reading a book prior to his visit to the bathroom, when he never read any books?

When author Norris interviewed some of Loewenstein's friends much later, several indicated straight out that they felt Loewenstein had been murdered, and one specifically said that Baxter did it. No proof, but interesting, we'll call them unsupported assertions.

After Loewenstein's death, Baxter who appeared to live well also became valet to Loewenstein's son, Robert, who was 18 years of age. Robert, unlike his father, was a playboy and enjoyed a merry social life.

One April day in 1932, Baxter visited Robert's apartment where something strange happened. Robert told police that he left his apartment but when he returned later he found a note on the front door, which was locked. The note read, "Don't come in. Go and stay with the Countess." The Countess, most likely was Anna Carolina Minici, who lived with her husband, next door to Robert.

Robert maintained that he gained access to his own apartment by way of his neighbor's residence. He told the police that he found Baxter lying on the floor and that he had been shot. A small revolver, which belonged to Robert, was lying on the floor nearby. Baxter died a few hours later; his autopsy showed an abnormal amount of alcohol in his body. He also left a short "goodbye" letter to Robert; however, it did not reveal anything about why he might have taken his own life.

Baxter and Robert seemed to have a palsy-walsy relationship. What was that all about? Did Baxter at some point tell Robert what happened to his father? Or, did he take whatever he knew to his grave?

It is likely that some one paid off Baxter and Hodgson for their part in the larger conspiracy, and that they did not carry out the murder by themselves. Interestingly enough, Hodgson seemed to vanish after the death of Loewenstein.

We feel that the two women stenographers, who apparently were recently hired, did not participate in any physical way in Loewenstein's murder. They were, however, also paid off and told to keep quiet and vanish, which they did.

Pilot Perfidy

At the preliminary inquiry Drew and Little said that Loewenstein could have easily opened the exit door on the plane, but when questioned later they seemed to be not quite so certain about what they said earlier. As we have noted, experiments carried out by others concluded that one man could have only opened the exit door only slightly. Were Drew and Little's comments the beginning of a cover up?

Furthermore, Drew never gave a clear answer why he landed on a deserted beach and not landed at a nearby aerodrome where the Coast Guard could have been notified to begin to search for Loewenstein. Also, why didn't Drew use his two-way radio to communicate with anyone?

Drew had the reputation of being a womanizer and also one who enjoyed having and spending money. After Loewenstein's death, Drew lived in a luxurious apartment and continued to live extremely well all the rest of his life—well beyond the salary an airline pilot earns. Where did he get all that money?

Drew's companion, Little, was also an interesting case. He said that Loewenstein took off his jacket, collar and tie before going to the bathroom; however, the jacket was never found on the plane but the collar and tie were. After the plane landed, Little picked up some notes that were scattered about on the floor, which Loewenstein wrote before disappearing. It's strange that Little never showed them to anyone, but he gave them to his wife Julie. When Norris spoke with Julie (after her husband had died), he managed to get copies of the notes, but there was no smoking gun there; Loewenstein's notes essentially related to his business enterprises. But why didn't Little turn over the notes to the authorities when he found them?

Little also prospered after Loewenstein's death. He had an aviation consultancy business at an upbeat address in London, and also had a luxurious apartment in Paris. His new found wealth was also suspicious.

Norris, to his credit, doggedly tracked down a number of people that he interviewed for his book. In his conversation with Julie, she told Norris that all the crew was guilty--but gave no specific names.

Loewenstein had his share of enemies in the vicious and competitive business world that was his entire life, and there were some who would have profited greatly by his death. We propose that those men, greedy for money and with power and influence, chose Drew and Little as the most reliable to carry out Loewenstein's murder.

We think that it is highly probable that Drew and Little, and most likely with some help from the two valets, physically managed to toss Loewenstein from his own plane out into the sky and to his death. We conclude that Drew and Little, who liked money and were well paid, were the main culprits in the conspiracy in Loewenstein's death. All six on the plane, however, were paid off, since money was no problem.

Recommended Reading

Norris, William. *The Man Who Fell From the Sky*. Haines City, Florida. SynergEBooks, 2000.

One Missing from the Long Gray Line

As you're cruising up the mighty Hudson River, about 50 miles north of New York City, you look up at stately West Point, located on the western bank of the river. The country's most esteemed military academy, sits staunchly on scenic high ground overlooking the misty Hudson Valley. The picturesque campus's neogothic buildings, made of somber gray or black granite, rank among the most attractive in the country.

The Academy, which traces its rich history back to the Revolutionary War, has provided America with many top commanders and famous personalities including, Ulysses S. Grant, Robert E. Lee, George Armstrong Custer, John Pershing, Dwight Eisenhower, Douglas MacArthur and many others.

On the evening of January 14, 1950, a wintry chill hovers over the Academy. Richard Cox, a bright, handsome West Point cadet, is getting dressed formally after receiving an invitation for dinner at the grand Hotel Thayer on a hilltop on the campus grounds. The male visitor Cox was going to have dinner with had visited him twice the previous week. He was someone Cox knew from the time they both served in an army intelligence unit in Germany. It all seemed so innocent, just another Saturday night out as Cox leaves around 6:15 p.m. and tells his roommate that he will be back early that evening.

In 1950, a team of 11 thieves steals almost three million dollars (equivalent to about $29 million in 2014) in the Brink's robbery in Boston, President Harry Truman orders the development of the hydrogen bomb, the Korean War begins and there is an assassination attempt on President

Truman by Puerto Rican nationalists. People are listening to "Goodnight Irene," by Gordon and the Weavers and Nat King Cole's "Mona Lisa," while "Cinderella" is a smash Walt Disney movie. And the first modern credit card is introduced.

Cox, however, did not go to the Hotel Thayer and he never returned to his room. He just vanished without a trace while still on the hallowed grounds of America's legendary military academy. He is the only cadet who has disappeared and never found—dead or alive.

It seemed as though he passed through a portal into another dimension. His puzzling disappearance ranks with those of Judge Crater, Amelia Earhart and Jimmy Hoffa.

Background

Richard Colvin Cox was born on July 25, 1928 in Mansfield, Ohio. He was ten years old when his father died; however, his mother dutifully carried on and operated the family insurance business. While he participated in various extra-extracurricular activities, he was also an excellent student and graduated with honors from Mansfield High School in 1946.

Cox enlisted in the army after graduating from high school and did his basic training at Fort Knox, Kentucky. He was then sent to Coburg and later Schweinfurt, in Germany where he served in the S-2 (intelligence) section of a military police unit that patrolled the border between East and West Germany.

After he was promoted to the rank of sergeant, he applied and was accepted for admission to West Point. Meanwhile, his protective mother was able to get him a congressional appointment to the Academy; however, he would have preferred to get accepted on his own merit. He left Germany in January 1948 and attended West Point's Preparatory School at Steward Field, and then entered the Academy in July.

First year students are known as "plebes," and sometimes they have a difficult time adjusting to the rigorous discipline and academic life at the Academy. On occasion the pressure becomes so overwhelming that a cadet leaves without permission, but they usually return and serve out their punishment and are accepted back to the ranks.

Cox's first year went well, however, he did experience the typical difficulties that other plebes faced. In September 1949, he started his sophomore year and shared a room with cadets Deane Welch and Joseph Urschel. After the first 18 months, Cox had an excellent academic record and also was an outstanding member of the Academy's intercollegiate Track and Cross Country team.

While at home for the Christmas holidays, he and his girlfriend Betty Timmons discussed eloping, which was surprising since that meant expulsion from West Point, but the conversation ended there.

On January 5, 1950, after returning to the Academy, he wrote to his mother complaining about cadet life, but the letter was generally positive. Then on January 7, he wrote her again talking about his future marriage and how fortunate she will be to have a wonderful daughter-in-law.

But, then, on that very Saturday afternoon, a strange phone call for him started a series of unusual events that led to his shocking and puzzling disappearance. ("*Oblivion,*" by Harry J. Maihafer,)

The Mysterious "George" Shows Up

On Saturday, January 7, 1950, at 4:45 p.m., Cadet Peter C. Hains, in Charge of Quarters at Company B, received a telephone call. A man in a rough speaking voice asked if Dick Cox was in the company. When Hains told the caller he was, the man then said tell him to come down to the hotel, which was on the Academy grounds. Also, tell him "George" called; we met when we were in German together, and I would like to have dinner with him. Hains then put the message in Cox's mailbox in the orderly room.

Around 5:15 p.m., Cox picked up his telephone message and went back to his room. A little later, the civilian caller went to the reception room where he met Cadet Mauro Maresca, who was the reception officer, and asked to see Cox. Maresca contacted Cox, but before leaving his room Cox told his roommate Welch that his visitor was someone he met in Germany, but was vague about mentioning his name.

Cox met his visitor at Grant Hall where they talked for a while. Maresca overheard Cox telling George that he would have to change into full dress in order to eat at Thayer Hotel. It was around 5:40 p.m. when Cox and his visitor left Grant Hall. George then invited Cox to his car where he shared a bottle of whiskey with him; surprisingly, Cox got drunk.

Cox then returned to his room, however, he never went to the Thayer Hotel for dinner, but gave his word that he was going to when he signed the departure slip initially at 1923 (7:23 p.m.). Joe Urschel, his other roommate, returned from supper and started to write some letters. About 7:15 p.m., Cox entered his room with only a towel wrapped around him, having just showered. Shortly afterward, Cox also began to write a letter but then fell asleep.

When the bugle call sounded at 9:30 p.m. that night, Cox suddenly woke up and rushed out into the hallway. He seemed confused and called out something that sounded like he was looking for someone named "Alice." While his roommates were ushering him back to his room, they finally realized he had returned drunk after his visit with his friend George.

The next morning Cox appeared to be himself. He told his roommates that his visitor brought a bottle of whiskey and insisted that he drink with him while sitting in his car. Cox then made a strange remark saying that George made him promise that he would see him the next day. Cox left around noon on Sunday to meet his friend and returned about 5:00 p.m. He complained that the man wasted his entire weekend when he had planned to study.

Over the next several days, Cox told his roommates that his visitor was a ranger who enjoyed bragging about killing Germans during the war. George also said that he got a German girl pregnant and then murdered her to prevent her from giving birth to the child. It seemed like a strange thing for Cox to say; but then, it was also somewhat unusual that Cox never referred to his visitor by name.

Meanwhile, Cox deliberately changed his initial departure time from 1923 (7:23 p.m.) to 1823 (6:23 p.m.) to make it appear that he attended the 6:30 p.m. dinner formation at the mess hall on Saturday evening, although he did not. Trivial as this might seem to us, it was a serious offense at West Point.

One week later, on Saturday afternoon January 14, Cox and Welch attended a basketball game on the post. Sometime later after the game, as they approached the cadet barracks, Cox told Welch to go on since he wanted to check his grades, which were posted weekly.

Shortly afterward, Cadet John Samotis saw Cox talking to a civilian, who for all intent and purposes was the man who visited Cox the previous week. Since Cox had a visitor, he could miss the evening meal at the mess hall and have dinner with his friend at Hotel Thayer. Cox then signed the departure slip 1745 (5:45 p.m.).

Cox returned to his room and told Welch that his friend who had visited him the previous week had invited him for dinner at the hotel. About 6:15 p.m., as Welch was leaving for his evening meal at the mess hall, he told Cox that he would see him later. Cox, who was attired in formal dress, told Welch that he would be back early—around 9:00 or 9:30 p.m. Cox gave the appearance that it was just another Saturday night out.

Cox did not go to the Thayer Hotel and more seriously he did not return to his room when taps sounded at 11:00 p.m., which cadets are required to do. Cadets escorting a date to a hop, however, were given an extra hour to sign in. Shortly after midnight, all cadets were signed in--but next to Cox's name, the space to sign in was blank—Cox had not returned.

For over six decades, his mysterious disappearance has baffled everyone to this very day. (*"Oblivion,"* Harry J. Maihafer,)

Lavish Leads

When Cadet Lou Bryan, who was in charge of quarters on Saturday night, January 14, did not find Cox in his room after a final inspection, he notified his superior that Cox was missing. By mid-morning of the next day all the senior officers in various departmental units were notified that Cox was absent without leave.

About 10:00 a.m., Major Henry Harmerling, Jr., called Mrs. Rupert Cox to inform her that her son, Richard, was missing. After awhile, he asked if Cox had contacted her, but unfortunately she said that he had not.

His two roommates were interviewed thoroughly, but they could not account for his strange disappearance. Shortly afterward, the word quickly got around to all the cadets that Cox went missing. There was a room-by-room search of all the buildings on the grounds and then the search proceeded to the entire surrounding area. A circular was prepared with his description and other information and sent to the press and law enforcement agencies throughout the east. Ponds and lakes in the area were not only dragged, but also drained.

Investigators interviewed his mother and two sisters along with his girlfriend. They contacted everyone they could think of who might know anything meaningful, but the came up with nothing.

The army called in the FBI who sent out information on Cox throughout the country. They questioned all soldiers who had known him prior to the time he entered West Point, but all that led nowhere. Their search in the United States drew a blank.

The army's Criminal Investigation Command (CID) investigators in Germany talked with every soldier that was acquainted with Cox, but nothing suspicious turned up. And, an exhaustive search for the mysterious "George" person did not turn up anything either.

Once the story of Cox went out to the media, there were many reported sightings of him in different places. His disappearance quickly captured the public's attention, which was expected. There are those who want to play cop, seek attention, or for whatever reason feel compelled to call the authorities with information that in most cases only leads to blind alleys and to dead ends. All leads were pursued; however, while some looked promising, there was no proof that Cox was out there somewhere. Author

Harry J. Maihafer, in his book *Oblivion,* describes all these sightings in fascinating detail.

Every aspect of his life was gone over carefully looking for some clue. He never contacted any member of his family, girlfriend, or any very close friends. It was a very confusing case, since every path seemed to run into a stonewall. Although an extensive and thorough search was carried out, there was no smoking gun. What's more, the barrel of the gun wasn't even warm.

There were, however, rumors about homosexuality, abduction, murder, suicide, CIA, Russian spies and running away. Let's look at some of the theories. ("The Devil's Right Hand: The Vanished Cadet," by Troy Taylor. Online article, January 7, 2013.)

Theories

Abduction

The year, 1950, was a red-letter year for Cold War incidents. The Russians shot down a U.S. Navy plane with ten men aboard over the Baltic Sea. It's possible that the ten-man crew, which was presumed dead and not found, were captured and never returned. In 1993, retired Russian General Fyodor Shinkarenko said that he believed the wreckage was secretly salvaged and sent to Moscow. It was also a time when a number of kidnappings took place in various Eastern Bloc countries. The Korean War broke out. And Joseph McCarthy, U.S. senator, started his "witch hunt" for Communists in the U.S. government.

Under the Freedom of Information Act, Marshall Jacobs (more on him later) managed to obtain a document titled, "American Prisoner at Vorkuta Camp USSR," which was dated May 24, 1957 and released on January 25, 1983.

The document affirmed: (a) That an American prisoner named Cox was being held at Vorkuta Camp, USSR; (b) That Cox did disappear from

West Point; (c) That on December 18, 1956, the American prisoner at Vortuka bore a striking resemblance to Richard Cox at the Academy and (d) That army intelligence had forwarded the enclosed information to the Commandant at West Point.

The prison at Vorkuta, which was located approximately 50 miles north of the Arctic Circle, held about 8,000 political prisoners.

There were some who felt that Cox was actually pirated out of the Academy. According to Jacobs, one such person was a freelance writer who spent considerable time at the library at West Point. He told the librarian that he believed Cox was abducted from the Academy. He was then put on board the Polish ship *Batory*, and transported to a Siberian prison for espionage against the Soviets when he served in the army in Germany. Cox went missing on January 14, while the *Batory* sailed out on January 20.

Jacobs, who was tenacious, diligently pursued this lead. There was a young American named Cox who was a prisoner at the Vorkuta Camp in the Soviet Union in the 1950s. He was released in 1954 and is now deceased. That person, however, was not Richard Colvin Cox. While Jacobs eventually felt that this story was unreliable, he pointed out that it was difficult to explain the 1956 sighting of Cox in the document.

We decided to include this story because it is weird and wild, however, it still falls within the realm of possibility since his body has never been found. We hasten to add, however, that this scenario is not very likely.

He Chose to Leave

About six months before he entered West Point, Cox wrote to his mother from Germany expressing strong negative feelings about the army and that he did not want to go to the Academy. Was this an omen or just a sense of uncertainty that a young man had about a major change in his life?

When he was home for the Christmas holidays shortly before his disappearance, he and his girlfriend Betty Timmons discussed eloping and going to Kentucky to get married. They actually started out driving to the

Blue Grass State, but decided that they would put off their marriage until after he graduated.

In the last several letters Cox sent to his mother, he complained a great deal about cadet life. In one letter he even asked her what she would think if he left West Point? In an unfinished letter to his girlfriend, he expressed an unusual feeling of anger and hatred for the Academy. He drew a face spitting on the words "United States Military Academy," on the letterhead of the West Point stationery.

We feel that while his griping about the rigor and discipline of military life was more than normal, it wasn't so serious that he would leave the Academy solely for that reason.

His life, though, appeared to be going well following the typical rigorous freshman year. Cox was in his mid-sophomore year and ranked in the upper one-third of his class. He was shaping up to be an excellent officer, which he always wanted to be. Furthermore, Cox and his girlfriend were engaged and they always chatted about their future life together. There did not appear to be anything serious to indicate he would simply leave West Point and vanish.

So it seems extremely unlikely he would have left the Academy and never contacted his mother, girlfriend, other family members or his closest friends. But we return to the idea of special circumstances that might lead to a voluntary disappearance below.

CIA

Cox's friend, George, clearly was the key to unlocking the mystery of his disappearance. Surprisingly, George, who served in the army with Cox in Germany, was never identified.

In his book, *Oblivion*, Author Maihafer incorporated the significant research carried out independently by Marshall Jacobs on Cox's disappearance. We commend Jacobs, who was a retired history teacher, for his wonderfully thorough research on such a complex case.

In *Oblivion*, Maihafer writes that Cox left West Point secretly and joined the Central Intelligence agency (CIA). He maintains that Cox chose this secret role and new life, and did not want to be found. Moreover, he carried on as an undercover agent until his death.

While this theory portrays Cox in an honorable role, serving his country in a patriotic manner, it is not very plausible. Why would he choose to lead a covert life and never contact anyone—not even a dying mother? Could he not have served his country equally honorably by graduating from the most prestigious military academy in the world? Although we do not doubt Jacobs' sincerity, his unnamed CIA source spins a tale that is just too fantastic.

We conclude that leading a cloak and dagger life, while interesting and exciting, is more a fanciful story.

Murder

There was no evidence to indicate that Cox knew that his friend George was coming to visit him. George's brusque manner, however, gave the impression that he was a domineering person who wanted things to go his way, rather than someone coming for a pleasant visit with a former colleague. Did George have something else he wanted to accomplish—a plan he had devilishly worked out?

It is difficult to understand why Cox would get drunk close to his barracks at the Academy when George visited him the first time. Cox told his roommates that George was insistent that he drink whiskey with him, but that doesn't excuse Cox's irresponsibility. Then later on, Cox chose to change the time on his departure slip, which was a major offense and could have caused him to be expelled from West Point.

It's also strange that Cox never revealed George's name; it was always "he," "him," or "my friend." Cox did, however, tell his roommates that his friend was a former Ranger and bragged about killing Germans. Cox also said that his friend told him that he got a German girl pregnant and then killed her to prevent her from giving birth to the child. No records, however, were found to substantiate that story, but that does not mean that it did not happen. Or was there some other secret serious offense they both harbored?

George might have been getting more concerned about some evil thing he did in their earlier relationship in Germany that only Cox knew about. Did Cox, perhaps, say things when he was drunk that gave George some concern to be alarmed? While one might question why George waited several years to take any action, he knew only too well the old adage, " Dead men tell no tales."

It's possible that George gave Cox something to drink, which had a pill in it to put him to sleep quickly or kill him, and then hastily put him in the trunk of his car and exited the gates.

This theory is not the most likely scenario, but a possible one.

Was He Gay?

It is of interest to note that the staff psychologist at West Point stated that Cox's visitor, George, was probably a "homosexualist." Maihafer also pointed out that there was anecdotal evidence that suggested Cox was gay. Furthermore, there were several men who stated emphatically that they had sex with Cox. These sexual relations allegedly took place during the time Cox was stationed at Stewart Field and also when he was a cadet.

Then one day his roommate, Urschel, received several letters from Greenwich Village suggesting that a man named George was involved in a homosexual relationship with Cox, which he turned over to the authorities. Were these simply "crank letters" by someone playing a sick joke? If it were proven that Cox was gay, it could have resulted in his dismissal from the Academy and also dishonored by other cadets as well. Was this why he disappeared?

Cox's roommates, however, stated emphatically that they had never observed anything that would indicate that Cox was gay. His family, girlfriend and all his close friends also felt that he was not gay.

Cox's so-called friend, George, appeared to be not only unsavory but possibly one who had a dark side. Their three meetings were not only curious but also mystifying. George seemed to have some influence over Cox when he visited him. Why would Cox jeopardize his career by getting drunk and also being dishonest in changing the departure time he recorded when he left for dinner with George on Saturday, January 7?

When Cox left for dinner on Saturday, January 14, Urschel said that his impression was that Cox had no intention of leaving the Academy—but he did. What caused him to change his mind? Cox and George, however, might have had a homosexual relationship. It's possible that he left with George to avoid any embarrassment to himself and his family. If he left willingly, he needed to get past the guard who checks the cars as they leave the gates. Did Cox simply hide within the car or did he choose to hide in the trunk? This is the only reason we can think of why Cox would not have contacted his family if he were alive.

On the other hand, we think it was more likely that it was a homosexual relationship that went wrong and that George had killed Cox. In that case, George most likely would have put him in the trunk of his car as he exited the gates. For George, it would not have been his first killing. He most likely would have chosen to toss his body (perhaps weighed down) into the Hudson River, which eventual drifted out into the ocean.

We conclude that Cox was gay, but that he did not leave willingly. Something went wrong in their relationship and George killed him.

Recommended Reading

Maihafer, Harry J. *Oblivion: The Mystery of West Point Cadet Richard Cox.* Washington, D.C., Brassey's Inc. 1996. This is a captivating book that we highly recommend.

Taylor, Troy. "The Devil's Right Hand: The Vanished Cadet," Online article, January 7, 2013.

An Unknown Civil Rights Pioneer

On a chilly, rainy evening in March 1939, a 28-year-old African-American graduate student leaves his fraternity house to go out on a quick errand to simply purchase some stamps. He steps out into the wind and rain, turns up the collar of his jacket, and walks briskly out into the streets of south Chicago. He vanishes without a trace—never to be seen or heard from again.

That young man was Lloyd Gaines, not a household name; however, he was involved in one of the most important U.S. Supreme Court cases in decades.

It's also the year that World War II starts, the deadliest conflict in human history. Franklin Delano Roosevelt, 32nd President of the United States, is in his second term. The New York World's Fair opens. The movie of the year, *Gone With the Wind* premieres. Unemployment is over 17% and the cost of a first-class stamp is only three cents.

Several years earlier in 1936, the United States was in its deepest and longest economic downturn in history. While the entire country suffered, no group was hit harder than African-Americans. That year, Gaines, who was academically qualified, was denied admission to the University of Missouri School of Law.

The case went to trial and then to the Missouri Supreme Court where he was still denied admission. The case then went to the U. S. Supreme Court, which ordered Missouri to admit Gaines to the all-white law school or provide an equal law school for African-Americans within the state.

After his supreme victory, Gaines went to Chicago to look for work. Less than three months later, he mysteriously slipped into the shadows and also into obscurity. His bewildering disappearance that cold, stormy night in Chicago was the beginning of a 75-year-old mystery that still haunts us today.

Background

Lloyd Gaines was born to sharecropper parents in Water Valley, Mississippi in 1911. In 1926, when he was fourteen, his father died and his mother, Callie, moved to St. Louis with her family (accounts vary from five to twelve regarding the number of children in her household).

Gaines was an excellent student and graduated first in his class at Vashon High School. After being awarded a $250 (equivalent to $3500 in 2014) scholarship in an essay contest, he attended Lincoln University in Jefferson City, Missouri. He was a member of Alpha Phi Alpha fraternity, a talented debater, and also president of his senior class. Gaines graduated with a B.A. degree in history. He also earned a M.S. degree in economics from the University of Michigan.

Gaines was regarded by those who knew him as quiet, strong-minded and a person who always kept to himself. He was held in high regard and was resolute about standing up for what he felt was right. He was, however, something of a loner, and at times would go off for days without letting anyone know where he was going.

Gaines was determined to improve his status in life even though the Great Depression and segregation were major obstacles for him to overcome. He always wanted to be a lawyer; however, that was not meant to be. He did, unknowingly, and somewhat reluctantly, become a civil rights pioneer.

Litigation Issues

First Trial

In 1935, when Gaines applied to the University of Missouri Law School, he was denied admission on racial grounds. Missouri, which was a segregation state, had a policy that would pay the tuition for African-Americans to study law in a nearby state since there was no separate law school for them in Missouri. Gaines, however, chose to decline the university's offer to pay his tuition at another out-of-state law school and filed suit.

Gaines and his attorneys, Sidney Redmond and Charles Houston, decided to center their argument on the "equal" part of the U.S. Supreme Court's 1896 *Plessy v. Ferguson* decision "separate but equal."

Houston chose to focus on segregation in the graduate and professional schools of state universities. The complete absence of graduate and professional opportunities in many states made the inequality dramatic and impossible to dismiss. "Not a single state-supported institution of higher learning in anyone of seventeen states out of nineteen states" enforcing separation by law allowed a Negro "to pursue professional or graduate training at public expense." ("Before Brown: Charles H. Houston and the Gaines Case," Douglas. O. Linder. Online article 2000.)

Houston argued that denying Gaines admission to the University of Missouri Law School on racial grounds was a violation of his constitutional rights.

William Hogsett, the state's attorney, argued that Gaines was a well-qualified student with the right to attend law school provided it was another school outside the state of Missouri. He also stated that it was public policy codified in the state constitution that African-American students not be admitted to the University of Missouri Law School.

In 1936, Judge Dinwiddie decided the case in favor of the state of Missouri; however, he did not explain his opinion in writing.

Missouri Supreme Court

Gaines appealed his case to the Missouri Supreme Court.

Houston argued that the refusal to admit Gaines to the University of Missouri violated his rights under the equal protection clause of the Fourteenth Amendment. Neither the "slender hope" that Gaines might someday attend a new law program at Lincoln nor the provision of tuition scholarships to attend an out-of-state law school met the Constitution's requirement of equal treatment regardless of race. ("Before Brown: Charles H. Houston and the Gaines Case," Douglas. O. Linder. Online article 2000.)

[Justice William Frank stated that] Missouri did not violate the separate-but-equal principle of Plessy: "Equality is not identity of privileges." Gaines can be adequately prepared for Missouri practice in an out-of-state school. His added travel costs to out-of-state schools "furnishes no substantial ground for complaint." Justice Frank concluded for the Court: [W].e hold that the opportunity offered appellant for law education in the university of an adjacent state is substantially equal to that offered white students by the University of Missouri." ("Before Brown: Charles H. Houston and the Gaines Case," Douglas. O. Linder. Online article 2000.)

In early 1937, the Missouri Supreme Court affirmed Judge Dinwiddie's decision.

U.S. Supreme Court

Houston and Redmond appealed to the U.S. Supreme Court. The *Gaines v. Canada* case was argued before the Court in November 1938.

Houston argued that the state's offer to pay Gaines to attend law school out-of-state could not guarantee him a legal education equal to that offered white students.

Chief Justice Charles Evans Hughes announced the Court's decision in *Missouri ex rel. Gaines v Canada*, Registrar of the

University of Missouri on December 12, 1938. The Missouri Supreme Court had erred. Missouri had violated the right of Lloyd Gaines to the equal protection of the laws. "The equal protection of the laws is a pledge of the protection of equal laws," Hughes declared. "The obligation of the state to provide the protection of equal laws must be performed . . . within its own jurisdiction." "The essence of the constitutional right is that it is a personal one." Gaines "as an individual" was entitled to have Missouri "furnish within its borders facilities for legal education substantially equal to those which the State afforded for persons of the white race, whether or not other Negroes sought the same opportunity." ("Before Brown: Charles H. Houston and the Gaines Case," Douglas. O. Linder. Online article 2000.)

In summary, the U.S. Supreme Court ordered the State of Missouri either to admit Gaines to the University of Missouri School of Law or to provide another school of equal status within the state borders.

An Open Road to Law School

In the spring of 1939, the breakthrough for Gaines to attend the University of Missouri Law School appeared, at last, to become a reality.

When the Missouri legislature, however, learned of the U.S. Supreme Court decision, they went into action. They chose to accept setting up a separate law school for African-Americans, rather than admitting Gaines to the University of Missouri Law School. The Missouri legislature passed a bill allocating $278,000 (equivalent to $4.7 million in 2014) to remodel an old beauty school, which would become Lincoln University Law School in Jefferson City. The National Association for the Advancement of Colored People (NAACP), which supported Gaines quickly planned to challenge the proposed new law school approved by the Missouri legislature.

Meanwhile, Gaines traveled about in Missouri, Kansas, and Illinois looking for work. While jobs of any kind were far and few between, it was even more difficult for African-Americans to find work. Gaines took any odd job he could get; he even gave talks to NAACP chapters and various churches for small donations. On numerous occasions, he had to borrow money from his brother, George, to get by.

During the time when he worked as a clerk for the Works Progress Administration (WPA) in Michigan, he earned a master's degree in economics from the University of Michigan. He then returned to Missouri since the NAACP was anticipating that new proceedings in his case would likely begin sometime soon.

Gaines then managed to get a job at a gas station in St Louis. When he learned that the proprietor was selling a low-grade fuel as premium petrol, he quit his job since he didn't want to be involved in the fraudulent practice if the authorities found out what was going on. Gaines then took the train to Kansas City where he gave a talk to the local NAACP chapter. He looked around for work in the city but was unable to find anything. Gaines left Kansas City and headed off on another train to Chicago.

Gaines Goes Missing

In early March, when Gaines finally settled in at Chicago, he sat down and wrote his last letter to his mother. At 5:00 p.m. on March 4, 1939, Gaines mailed her an eight-page letter from the Stock Yards Station in Chicago. The letter in part read:

> Dear Mother,
> I have come to Chicago hoping to find it possible to make my own way. I hope by this letter to make very clear to you the reasons for such a step...
> As for publicity relative to the university case, I have found that my race still likes to applaud, shake hands, pat me on the

back and say how great and noble is the idea, how historical and socially significant the case but—and there it ends. Off and out of the confines of publicity columns, I am just a man—not one who has fought and sacrificed to make the case possible, one who still is fighting and sacrificing—almost the 'supreme sacrifice' to see that it is a complete and lasting success for thirteen million Negroes—no! -- just another man. Sometimes I wish I were a plain, ordinary man whose name no one recognized.

I enjoyed my brief stay in K. C., but finding no possible opening for work there I decided to come over here. I found Eddie Mae Page at home and had her cook lunch—ham and eggs, wheat cakes and coffee. She had some of her chums come over and so I stayed until Mrs. Paige came in from work before getting a room at the 'Y.'

So far I haven't been able to dig up a single job prospect, but I'm still trying. Paid up my room rent until March 7th. If nothing turns up by then, I'll have to make other arrangements. Should I forget to write for a time, don't worry about it, I can look out for myself OK. As ever, Lloyd.

("Before Brown: Charles H. Houston and the Gaines Case," Douglas. O. Linder. Online article 2000.

While in Chicago, Gaines met Nancy Page and her daughter Eddie Mae. Since they were Gaines' former neighbors in St. Louis, they frequently invited him for dinner. Nancy said that sometime around mid-March, Gaines gave her the impression that he seemed "to be running away from something." He also told her that he got a job at a department store. It turned out that Gaines never showed up for the first day of employment at the store.

On March 17, 1939, on a chilly, rainy night in Chicago, Gaines left his fraternity house and casually told the house attendant that he was just going out to buy some stamps. Gaines went out—and never returned. He just vanished.

What Happened to Gaines?

It was known that Gaines was something of a loner and kept to himself. Since it was not uncommon for him to leave for periods of time without notifying anybody, days passed before anyone realized he went missing that rainy night in Chicago.

Surprisingly, there was no official report of his disappearance made to the police in either Chicago or St. Louis. It was almost six months after he vanished before a serious search got underway. Meanwhile, rumors began circulating that he was murdered, committed suicide or disappeared voluntarily because he and his family were threatened.

When Houston and Redmond went looking for Gaines in August to argue their case at the Missouri Supreme Court rehearing, they couldn't find him. Redmond said that his family didn't seem overly concerned about his disappearance; furthermore, his family was not that helpful in trying to locate him.

By September, the new Lincoln University School of Law opened with 30 African-American students; however, Gaines never showed up. As a result, their case could not proceed without Gaines being present.

The story of his disappearance eventually got widespread attention in the media, and anyone with information was asked to contact the NAACP. There were the usual sightings that are always reported when someone goes missing: some said Gaines was spotted in New York City, while others reported that he was seen in Mexico City. Unfortunately, no helpful leads were ever received—he simply dropped out of sight. Unfortunately, no police department at the time undertook a formal investigation of Gaines' disappearance.

In an internal FBI memo dated May 10, 1940, John Edgar Hoover, Director of the Bureau of Investigation wrote that they were not investigating the Gaines' case.

In December 2013, we received the FBI file on Lloyd L. Gaines, which we requested under the Freedom of Information Act (FOIA). The following Hoover memos are from that file.

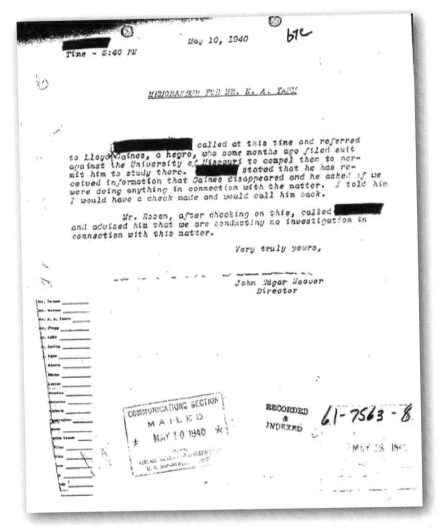

Thirty years later, in a letter dated May 13, 1970, Hoover stated that the case was not within the investigative jurisdiction of the FBI. It seems quite likely that Hoover simply had no interest in investigating it.

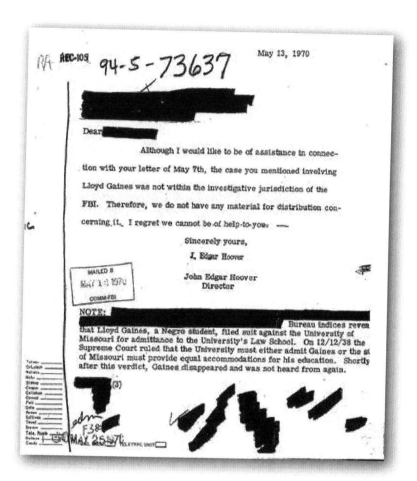

In early 1940, Missouri requested that the case before the state supreme court be dismissed since the plaintiff was absent. Houston and Redmond reluctantly had to agree and the motion was granted.

The NAACP spent $25,000 (equivalent to $422,000 in 2014) as well as a considerable amount of time on the Gaines' case. The NAACP leaders did not believe that Gaines had been abducted and killed, otherwise they would have called for an investigation. Historian Gary Lavergne noted that Gaines' lawyers Houston, Redmond and Thurgood Marshall (later appointed to the U.S. Supreme Court) also would have called for an investigation if they believed there was foul play. They, in fact, felt that Gaines had become resentful of the NAACP and disappeared on his own. Fifty years later, U.S. Supreme Court Thurgood Marshall unsympathetically told a reporter, "The sonaofabitch just never contacted us again." (Lloyd L. Gaines – Wikipedia, the free encyclopedia. Online article.)

Gaines' disappearance turned out to be a setback, since there were no other plaintiffs and funds were scarce. As a result, his case got pushed aside with the onset of World War II and other concerns. Meanwhile, Houston had resigned from the NAACP and was replaced by Thurgood Marshall. After the war, the NAACP moved forward with other plaintiffs and challenged segregationist policies in public graduate schools with other cases. By 1951 the University of Missouri School of Law finally admitted its first African-American student. In the mid 1950s, the Lincoln University School of Law closed since they had no students.

In 1954, *Brown v. Board of Education* overturned *Plessy v. Ferguson* ending the separate but equal doctrine. (More on this later.)

Follow-Up Investigations

Two media agencies, however, did choose to revisit the Gaines' case. *Ebony* magazine got involved in the 1950s and *The Riverfront Times*, a St. Louis weekly newspaper reexamined the Gaines' case almost seven decades later.

Ebony Magazine

In 1951, *Ebony* reporter Edward Clayton interviewed members of Gaines' family, some fraternity brothers and also a few of his close friends.

When Clayton spoke to his mother, Callie, she clearly gave him the impression that she and her son both felt that he would not follow through, and attend the University of Missouri Law School. She said that Gaines sent her a final postcard, which read "Goodbye. If you don't hear from me anymore you know I'll be all right."

When Clayton spoke with Gaines' brother, George, he said that Gaines felt the NAACP had exploited him. Furthermore, Gaines' family felt that the NAACP did not provide sufficient protection for him. Clayton said that George showed him the letters that Gaines wrote home. In his last letter, Gaines wrote that he was disappointed that he did not receive more support from civil rights organizations. His letter ended by saying he might be out of touch for a while.

When Clayton spoke with several Alpha Phi Alpha brothers, they stated that Gaines sent them postcards from Mexico; they were, however, unable to provide any of that correspondence.

Nancy Page told Clayton that when she asked Gaines if he planned on attending the University of Missouri law school, he said something to the effect: "If I don't go, I will have made it possible for another boy or girl to go." ("Lloyd L. Gaines" - Wikipedia, the free encyclopedia. Online article.)

The Riverfront Times

In 2007, reporter Chad Garrison of *The Riverfront Times* contacted George Gaines who was Lloyd's nephew. By that time all of Gaines' immediate family members and close associates had died. George stated that his family seldom spoke about Lloyd, but when they did it was always something positive. George said that he had assumed that his uncle had died, but only after reading *Ebony* did he learn about Lloyd's disappearance.

Garrison also communicated with Sid Reedy, a University City librarian, who also had a strong interest in Gaines' disappearance. Reedy told Garrison that he went to see Lorenzo Green, who was Gaines' mentor at Lincoln University. Green told Reedy that he made contact with Gaines when he visited Mexico in the late 1940s. Green maintains that he spoke to Gaines on the phone several times. While they made plans to have dinner together, Gaines never showed up. Greene told Reedy that Gaines simply had "grown tired of the fight . . . He had some business in Mexico City and apparently did well financially."

Garrison also reported that Green's son, Lorenzo Thomas Greene, said that his father told him about his contact with Gaines in Mexico. He added that his father, who was a civil rights activist, was reluctant to tell the FBI about his encounter with Gaines. He also said that his father hoped that Gaines would return to the United States.

Gaines' relatives had different views on what might have happened to him. Gaines great-niece, Paulette Mosby-Smith, was willing to accept the possibility that he went to Mexico. She said, " It's better than being buried in a basement somewhere—Jimmy Hoffa style." On the other hand, George Gaines told Garrison, "It's hard for me to believe that he went to Mexico and accepted a big payoff. That's not the same man who presented himself during the trial. I don't believe he would compromise his integrity like that."

Tracy Berry, another great-niece, who is a federal prosecutor, believes that Gaines was murdered. ("Lloyd L. Gaines" - Wikipedia, the free encyclopedia. Online article.)

FBI Reopens Cold Civil Rights Cases

In March 2007, the FBI stated that it would reopen over 100 cases of unsolved civil rights era killings in the South from 1952 to 1968. The NAACP then requested that the FBI also reopen the Gaines' case. Jeff Lanza, spokesman for the FBI in Kansas City stated that even though the Gaines' case did not fall with the specified dates, that the FBI would consider investigating the case.

By July 2012, the FBI did not initiate charges in any of the cases. It did, however, close all but 39 of the cases without recommending prosecution. On the other hand, it should be noted that these cold cases are difficult to solve. After a half century: evidence has been destroyed or lost; subjects and witnesses have either died or can't be located; memories have become clouded and faded and finally the original investigations did not have the technical and scientific advances used today.

The following three cases, which we briefly describe, were investigated by the FBI.

"Recy Taylor May Finally See Alabama Acknowledge Her 1944 Rape."

Recy Taylor was abducted and raped at gunpoint by seven white men in Abbeville, Ala., on Sept. 3, 1944. Her attack, one of un-counted numbers on black women throughout the Jim Crow era in the South, sparked a national movement for justice and an international outcry, but justice never came. Now, decades later, there may finally be some solace for Taylor, 91, as Alabama state Rep. Dexter Grimsley tries to make his state issue a formal apology. ("Recy Taylor may finally see Alabama acknowledge her 1944 rape," Ben Greenberg. Online article, March 17, 2011, The Civil Rights Cold Case Project.)

"FBI investigating Former Alabama Trooper for Another Killing"

The FBI continues to investigate former Alabama trooper James Bonard Fowler for yet another killing, the *Montgomery Advertiser* is reporting.

Last week, the 77-year-old former trooper pleaded guilty to second-degree manslaughter in the 1965 killing of Jimmie Lee Jackson in Marion, Alabama. That killing inspired the Selma-to-Montgomery march that played a pivotal role in the civil rights movement and helped to lead to the 1965 Voting Rights Act. Fowler will spend six months behind bars for the crime as part of his plea bargain.

But that bargain didn't include another killing that Fowler carried out, the 1966 killing of Nathan Johnson in Alabaster, Alabama. According to the *Montgomery Advertiser*, Johnson, 34, was arrested by Fowler for suspicion of drunken driving on May 8, 1966. Fowler said he shot Johnson because the suspect grabbed Johnson's billy club and began hitting him.

Credit for bringing attention to both of these forgotten killings goes to John Fleming, an editor at large with *The Anniston Star* who interviewed the former trooper in 2004. In that interview, Fowler admitted he had shot Jackson up to three times, claiming it was in self-defense. ("Journey to Justice," Jerry Mitchell. Online article, November 22, 2010.)

"Clifton Walker Case"

Clifton Walker had finished his late shift at International Paper in Natchez on Feb. 28, 1964 and was driving home to his wife and five children in southwest Mississippi when he took the shortcut he'd been warned against.

Driving alone in his 1961 cream-colored Chevrolet Impala, Walker decided, as he almost always did, to turn onto Poor House Road to save a circuitous mile on his way to Woodville, about 35 miles south of Natchez.

It was pushing close to midnight, it was dark and it was less than two weeks after 200 members of the Ku Klux Klan gathered in heat and anger at another southwest Mississippi town, Brookhaven. There they declared that the White Knights of the Ku Klux Klan would be a statewide organization, they agreed to a 40-page constitution that included "extermination" of blacks as a rational response to the growing civil rights threat, and they ignited dozens of cross burnings across the state.

Three hundred yards after turning onto Poor House Road, Walker was brought to a halt and, it appeared later, surrounded by men who began blasting away with shotguns.

Forty-five years later, no one has ever been charged in the murder of Clifton Walker. The FBI and Mississippi Highway and Safety Patrol appear in documents to have provided local prosecutors the names of two suspects against whom there was strong evidence, but nothing came of it. ("Clifton Walker Case." Online article, The Civil Rights Cold Case Project.)

Theories

Suicide

Unfortunately, some people who go missing do so with the intention of committing suicide. While Gaines did have a history of leaving for days without telling anyone, he would invariably show up later. No one really seemed to be overly concerned when he left on that rainy night in Chicago—but, then, he never returned.

Gaines appeared to be worried and distressed about something prior to his disappearance, but he never really confided completely in anyone. He always gave the impression that he wanted to work out issues and problems by himself.

Gaines clearly felt, however, that he was being manipulated by the NAACP and was disappointed in how they treated him. Did all the anxiety that was going on in his life at the time so traumatize him that he could not take it anymore? Was he so distraught by the pressures of fighting his case that he wanted to end it all?

We feel that while he might have been dissatisfied and discouraged by everything that was going on, he would not have resorted to such a drastic measure as suicide. He always had a positive attitude and not only wanted to improve his life, but wanted control his destiny. He felt that he had a life worth living and was determined to lead it his own way.

While suicide was a possibility, we feel strongly that it is not likely that he would have chosen to take his own life.

Murder

When someone goes missing and it's believed that foul play was involved, the case gets murky, especially when there is no body. While it is difficult to get rid of a body permanently, evil-minded people with a mission know their trade only too well. And even the less prepared can get lucky in finding a lonely burial spot—especially if more than one person is involved.

During the time period that Gaines lived, many states enforced segregation through "Jim Crow" laws. The states could impose legal punishments on people for "breaking" a wide variety of rigid anti-black laws.

Gaines undoubtedly angered many people when he applied to the University of Missouri Law School. The resentment against him became more serious as he continued to press his case in court all the way to the U.S. Supreme Court--and eventually won. After all, he almost single-handedly forced the state of Missouri to establish and start up a separate law school for African-American students.

Gaines certainly recognized that there would be bitterness against him. He was also aware that death threats against blacks were often followed up with lynching or burning bodies. Gaines, however, always felt that he could take care of himself. Nevertheless, as the rancor against him increased, a decision to eliminate him may have come to a point where strong action had to be taken; it may have been only a matter of when and where it would be carried out.

Perhaps the killers kept track of Gaines and went into action when he traveled to Chicago. Abducting Gaines and murdering him in another state would make it appear that it might have been a random killing rather than the work of racists. Furthermore, the hoodlums could have carried out their vicious crime at night, in the rain and when he was alone—all to their advantage.

We feel there is a strong possibility that racists murdered Gaines for his role in the civil rights movement.

Time to Move on

It isn't a crime for an adult to go missing. Adults frequently disappear for various reasons. Gaines also went missing, but what happened when he vanished without a trace that rainy windy night in Chicago? Let's look more closely at his personal life.

Gaines did not have an easy life growing up as a young African-American in a segregated world. He was, however, an excellent student who had a master's degree in economics and always wanted to be a lawyer. He was not a public person, but more a private individual and also complex.

When he applied for admission to the University of Missouri Law School, his life began to slowly change in unforeseen and complicated ways. All the legal controversy related to his being rejected by the law school seemed to cause him grief. It appeared that his personality was not suited to dealing with being the "point man" in a major civil rights case. There were times when he felt it would have been better to be anonymous, rather than being manipulated by the NAACP—as it seemed to him, rightly or wrongly--and constantly being before the public.

Gaines felt that he was not in control of his life, but that the civil rights issue was controlling him. He clearly resented the manner in which the NAACP was turning his life in a direction that he did not want to go. We think that he was overwhelmed with all the commotion and the long time it took to fight his case. He wanted to be in charge of his own life and control his own destiny.

Since Gaines and his family might have received death threats, their safety and his own could also have been a factor in his disappearance. We feel that Gaines eventually decided to start a new life for himself in Mexico. It's also likely he might have had some help in doing so. While it meant cutting all ties with his family, we feel that it was a deliberate and conscious decision he finally had to make. He was in the prime of his life, and if he was ever going to break away from all that clamor it was now--and alone if necessary.

We feel it's most likely that Gaines, with a heavy heart, decided that it was time to create a new life and a new identity. It might not have been the most heroic option, but it was a very human and understandable one.

Recommended Reading

"Lloyd L. Gaines" - Wikipedia, the free encyclopedia. Online article.

Honors

In 1995 the University of Missouri School of Law established a scholarship in his name. The school also named the first African-American center at the school for Gaines and another African-American student who also challenged the school's segregation policy in 2001. A portrait of Gaines hangs in a noticeable public place in the law school building.

In 2006, the law school awarded Gaines an honorary degree in Law. Furthermore, the state bar association granted him an honorary posthumous law license. At that time, Gaines would have been 95 years old if he were still alive.

Brown v. Board of Education of Topeka

On May 17, 1954 the United States Supreme Court handed down its ruling in the landmark case of *Brown v. Board of Education of Topeka*, Kansas. The Court's unanimous decision overturned provisions of the 1896 *Plessy v. Ferguson* decision, which had allowed for "separate but equal" public facilities, including public schools in the United States. Declaring that "separate educational facilities are inherently unequal," the *Brown v. Board* decision helped break the back of state-sponsored segregation, and provided a spark to the American civil rights movement. (*"Brown v. Board of Education of Topeka"* – History. com articles, video, pictures and facts. Online article.)

Brown v. Board of Education of Topeka is justly considered a landmark in our history of constitutional jurisprudence. *Missouri ex rel.Gaines v. Canada* is largely forgotten. Gaines deserves better. Of the two cases, only the outcome of Gaines was in genuine doubt. The Court's language in Gaines—the first Supreme Court victory ever achieved by blacks in an education case—required that States prove Negroes had real and substantial equality of educational opportunities. That language, coupled with a shift in attitudes concerning racial issues brought on by World War II, made the Court's verdict in Brown all but inevitable. ("Before Brown: Charles H. Houston and the Gaines Case," Douglas. O. Linder. Online article 2000.)

The story of Brown is well known. But it has overshadowed the pioneering cases and actors that were its indispensable precursors. Lloyd Gaines was essential to the legal strategy launched nearly two decades earlier that targeted higher education overall and legal education in particular. ("Robert Elias: Lloyd Gaines, a lost hero of civil rights," Robert Elias. The Cap Times, Online article, Copyright 2013.)

Found–but Still Lost

The Couple that Never Was

We weren't lovers, just brave strangers,
As we fought and we tumbled through the night.

"BRAVE STRANGERS" - BOB SEGER.

The young couple were indeed strangers in the area—and have remained so to this day. It was early in August of 1976 when they found themselves in Sumter County, South Carolina, the Palmetto State. They weren't in some small, quaint sleepy town but were traveling through a rural, lonely part of the county.

The girl was about 19 years of age and quite pretty. She was approximately five feet five inches tall and weighed 105 pounds. She had brown hair and hazel eyes with unusually long attractive eyelashes.

The young man was about six feet tall and weighed 150 pounds. He had brown hair and brown eyes. They were both dressed casually and had a clean-looking appearance.

No one knows if they had plans to stay in the region or were just passing through. Then one late summer day in August, the young couple was found murdered not far from Interstate 95 alongside a secluded dirt road that was lightly traveled. They weren't carrying any identification, but they were wearing expensive-looking jewelry.

The mystery of who they were, how they got there and how they lived is our final story. In our other stories, we know a lot about the people; we just don't know where they went. In our penultimate story, we consider the opposite possibility. We know where the young couple ended up, but that's all we know. In our other cases, men and women disappear into the mist and fog and their future is unknown. The young couple lying on a desolate roadside in Sumter County had no future and we have to enter the fog and mist to find who they are and where they came from.

But, then, how do you go about looking for two persons with no identity?

Slaying in Sumter County

A truck driver found the dead couple around 6:30 a.m., on August 7, 1976, approximately 25 miles east of Sumter, South Carolina. The bodies were found beside Locklair Road, a byway dirt road that connected Interstate 95 and S. C. 341 in Sumter County. When the police arrived on the scene, they quickly realized that the man and woman were both shot several times. They were not carrying any possessions: no money, identification, wallet or purse, and no alcohol or drugs. The only item found was a small box of Grant Truck Stop matches in the pants pocket of the man.

The man was judged to be in his 20s and was wearing faded blue jeans and a red T-shirt. "Coor's America's light beer" was printed on the front of the T-shirt and "Camel Challenger GT Sebring 75" across the back.

The attractive young girl was about 18 years of age and was wearing short blue jeans. She had a pinkish halter top that was fastened in the front and a light tan colored blouse. She was wearing wedge-heeled sandals with colorful straps. ("The Mystery Couple," Sharyn Lucas-Parker. Online article, Crime Library on truTV.com.)

They were, however, still wearing their jewelry. She wore three distinctive silver rings that had an American Indian or Mexican look. One ring had multi-colored stones, another was black and the third was jade colored.

The man was wearing a Bulova Accutron wristwatch. His ring was a 14 karat gold band with a gray star-shaped stone and engraved on the inside with the initials "JPF." If robbery was the motive, why not take the jewelry and watch?

The coroner's report stated that the couple had been shot at close range in the chest, throat and back: they had been dead for less than 24 hours. The report also showed that the couple ate some ice cream or fruit not very long before they were murdered. They were not sexually molested and neither one was wearing underwear. Both were white and had smooth olive-toned skin.

The man had two-inch scar marks on his right shoulder. He also had a substantial amount of expensive looking dental work done. The girl had a small beauty mark on her right cheek and two more small ones on her left cheek. Her legs were not shaven smooth: back then, most American girls shaved their legs.

The two bodies appeared to be killed quickly with little effort and just dumped on the shoulder of a rural, lonely road. They were shot with a .357-caliber handgun. According to retired Sumter County Chief Deputy Bobby McGhee, who was working as a uniform patrol-man close to the scene of the slayings that night, the killing occurred after midnight.

Why were they murdered? Who did the killing? And who were they?

Clueless

Even though the authorities could not identify the young couple, they were hopeful that they would be able to locate their families. They were, how-ever, frustrated since there were no solid clues or leads.

They concluded that the man's T-shirt most probably came from the 1975 Coors sponsored Sebring Races in Florida, and the box of matches most likely came from a Midwest truck stop. Researching the serial num-ber on the man's wristwatch and initials on the inside of his ring did not reveal anything meaningful. His dental charts were published nationwide, but they did not provide any clues as to his identity.

Nor did the girl's apparently distinctive rings lead anywhere. Their fingerprints were also checked out with negative results. The police followed every clue and exhausted all leads, but they came up with nothing.

Then four months after the murder, the authorities got their first significant lead. Lonnie George Henry was arrested on a suspected driving under the influence charge while traveling through Latta, North Carolina. When the police searched his vehicle, they found a .357-caliber handgun, which had some of the serial numbers filed off. When the State Law Enforcement Division (SLED) examined the weapon, they concluded that the bullets from the handgun matched those taken from the murdered couple.

("The Mystery Couple," Sharyn Lucas-Parker. Online article, Crime Library.)

A polygraph test showed that Henry did not always tell the truth, however, they were not able to place him at the site of the crime. Henry stated that he was visiting his wife in the hospital in North Carolina at the time, and he had witnesses to support his alibi.

When the police timed the drive from Sumter County to the hospital in North Carolina, they concluded that it would have taken Henry too long to complete the trip and they let him go. He was never charged with the killing. Henry was the only suspect the police had; he died in 1982.

Since the ballistics evidence seems solid, it appears that the handgun found in Henry's car was the murder weapon, but his alibi also seems credible. Did he take a murder secret to the grave? Or did he just get the gun from someone else?

Meanwhile, the investigation continued into the identity of the young couple and what they were doing in Sumter County. They were not wearing backpacks or had an unkempt appearance, which they might have had if they were hitchhiking across the country. While flyers and descriptions of the couple were circulated widely, no one reported to the police seeing them walking or hitchhiking.

Investigators pursued the idea that the couple might be from some-where outside the United States. They contacted U. S. Customs security and immigration officials as well as Interpol, but to no avail. The authorities found it difficult to believe that no family or anyone else was able to identify the couple. Who in the world were they? Their appearance and possessions show that they were at least from a middle-class background: they were clearly not part of the faceless long-time homeless population. Someone, somewhere should have missed them.

Months and months went by with no further leads. The authorities continued to work diligently to solve the case, but they came up with noth-ing. A year went by and still nothing turned up. Years passed and then many years went by with no resolution to the crime.

Sumter Coroner Verne Moore tried for years to get the case on na-tional television. Finally in 1995, a segment on "Unsolved Mysteries" and an investigation by "Court TV," as it was known then, did not turn up anything.

In 2008 Coroner Moore contacted a Montreal newspaper and *Reader's Digest French* and each wrote stories about the missing couple in South Carolina. About the same time, Constable Jim Gurney of the Edmonton Police Service, Alberta, Canada, learned of the murdered couple found in Sumter County. The Canadian authorities thought that the murdered couple in South Carolina might be a missing couple from Edmonton.

In 2009, the Edmonton Police Service sent a DNA sample of the miss-ing Canadian couple to the current Coroner Harvin Bullock at Sumter, South Carolina. Bullock then forwarded the DNA to a laboratory at the University of North Texas to see if it matched with the sample they had of the couple murdered in South Carolina. ("Couple Missing 1973 compared to 'Jacque and Jill' 1976 Sumter Co SC," Jason Wermers. Online article, August 25, 2009.)

We have contacted Harvin Bullock several times (most recently in 2013) about the DNA sample sent to him from the Edmonton Police, however, he has not responded to our correspondence. When we contacted Constable Jim Gurney, he informed us that he also has not heard anything in respect to the DNA they sent to Coroner Bullock. We presume, therefore, that there was no match.

We want to express our appreciation to Constable Gurney for his cooperation as well as the following information he sent to us. Gurney said, "We have now changed our rules in EPS Missing Persons Unit with respect to DNA as a result. We obtain our own DNA profiles through a lab, which we will then gladly pass along to any other agencies requesting a comparison with their found remains. Should anyone in Sumter County decide to contact us, we will gladly assist."

Why Were They Killed?

There was no authoritative order to round up suspects who might have killed the young couple, because there were no clues or leads that pointed to anyone. It was a baffling case from the very beginning since there was no starting point.

We'll begin by suggesting some possibilities that, while possible, are least likely. Was the couple involved with drugs in some manner? Their appearance, their apparent manner of traveling and where they were abducted and killed, did not see to connect to drug trafficking in any way. In short, there was nothing to support that theory.

Their deaths clearly did not display overkill, and there is no reason to think that the killer knew the victims or was seeking revenge. The couple was traveling in unfamiliar territory and they were strangers in the region. They were also strangers to those who murdered them.

While one might even consider that it was a random killing or a serial killer, it is much more likely that the couple appeared to be an easy prey for a robbery, especially by someone on drugs or who needed money. The young man and woman could have been picked up and taken to that desolate area where they were murdered.

It was not uncommon at the time that young people often wore backpacks while hitchhiking across the country, however, none were found at the site of the crime. But they could have been taken along with all their other possessions. It seems likely, though, that if they were hitchhiking someone should have seen them and reported it to the police, but no one did.

Let's assume that they had been picked up hitchhiking. It would have been difficult for one person to control two people, drive away to an isolated region and murder them. It is more likely that the couple was either picked or perhaps even abducted by two men and taken to that rural area and killed.

On the other hand, the couple could have been driving their own vehicle and were hijacked and then murdered. In this scenario, it is most likely that two men would have committed the crime. While disposing of the couple's car would have been a problem, murderers also knew how to get rid of a car.

While Lonnie George Henry was a strong suspect, the police eventually had to accept his alibi and let him go. Did Henry commit the crime, but managed to somehow get witnesses to support his alibi? The handgun found in his car, however, was akin to a smoking gun. While the handgun matched the bullets in the two dead bodies, the police were not able to determine who owned the gun. According to McGehee, the police were of the opinion that the handgun found in Henry's vehicle was the murder weapon. Even if Henry didn't pull the trigger, he may well have known who committed the crime.

Who Were They?

It's truly amazing that no one has come forward all these years and identified the young couple.

Let's start with the 19-year-old girl. If she had a family in this country, it's highly likely that someone would have come forward and identified her. And it's also reasonable (although perhaps a little less likely) that if she came from another country, someone would also have recognized her.

Recall, U.S Customs investigators, immigration officials and Interpol were notified about the dead couple.

Since it's difficult to comprehend that any family would not have come forward, she might not have had a typical family. She could have left an orphanage or similar institution several years ago, and since she didn't have any family chose not keep in touch with anyone. It is also possible that she might have had a lone family member or relative who reared her that died some years ago, leaving her completely alone.

On the other hand, it is more puzzling why the young man was not identified, since it appeared that he might have come from a reasonably well-to-do family. While his ring was initialed with the letters "JPF," it didn't lead to anything meaningful. It is surprising, however, that no dentist was able to identify his unusual dental work, since his dental charts were distributed widely across the nation as well as abroad.

Where was his family and why haven't the authorities heard from them? Was he so estranged from his family for years and had completely cut himself off from his past? Or did the last member of his family or a lone relative who might have reared him die off years ago leaving him with no one able to say who he was?

It is equally puzzling trying to determine where they came from as it is trying to identify them. While nothing can be ruled out, it appeared that the couple was not from the general area where they were murdered, and perhaps not from the southeastern part of the country since the media's reporting covered the story thoroughly.

Were they hitchhiking across the country? The girl's jewelry, which had an American Indian or Mexican look suggested that they might have traveled through the southwestern part of the country, or that they had been in Mexico. But then, those personal ornaments could have been purchased almost anywhere.

They were both white with olive-toned skin, but that doesn't tell us where they came from. They could have come from another country, but then, they could have been children of immigrant parents. There just wasn't anything concrete, which strongly suggested or pointed that they came from another country or not.

For almost 40 years, the search goes on, and the headline for the young couple, still reads:

NO LEADS, NO I. D., NO CLOSURE.

The young man and woman are buried in Bethel Methodist Church Cemetery in Oswego, Sumter County, South Carolina. Their bronze plaques read, "Male Unknown, August 9, 1976" and "Female Unknown, August 9, 1976."

In 2014, an online article stated that the following information came from Lt. Robert Burnish of the Sumter County Sheriff's Office.

1. "DNA testing has proven that John and Jane Doe were *NOT* siblings or otherwise related by blood.
2. There was not indication of European descent through DNA." ("Mystery of the Sumter County Does," by Sara Marie Hogg. Venture Galleries--Online article, February 3, 2014).

A Scenario for the Mystery Couple

In a puzzling case like this, no one can say with certainty who they were and why they were killed. It comes down to a matter of probabilities: one thing is more likely than another.

We think the young couple were Americans (there was no evidence of their entering the country) and that neither one had any recent contact with a typical family. In a way, they had no past in terms of someone coming forth not only to identify them, but to claim their bodies. So it isn't that strange that no one knows who they are.

The young lady most likely was an orphan for a number of years. After leaving the orphanage, she was alone in the world and in a way, a non-entity. Her companion was more likely reared in a family of above average income since he had expensive dental work done. A single parent who passed away when he was a young lad might have cared him for. He was then left alone without even any relatives. He was judged to be in his late 20s when he was killed, so he too, was orphan-like and without a family for many years.

When the two met, they immediately gravitated to each other since they had no ties to anyone. They had saved up some money and thought that it would be fun to travel across the country.

It was late summer and they were casually dressed, which is the way they traveled. They weren't overly concerned about their safety and perhaps gave the appearance of being too carefree. They were enjoying their life together, and likely stopped whenever they felt like taking a short break and then they would be off again.

The coroner's report revealed that they ate fruit or ice cream not long before they were murdered. Someone reported that they saw a young couple that matched the dead couple's description at a fruit stand in the general area, but were unable to determine if they were with others or if they had a car.

We suspect that one, but more likely two men saw the young couple at the fruit stand as someone easy to rob. By acting boldly at an opportune time, they completely surprised the couple by taking them hostage as well as hijacking their car. It was clearly much easier for two men to carry out this crime rather than one desperate criminal. We think the young couple had a car, since they were too well dressed and well kempt to have been living homeless or on the road.

The hijackers drove off to a secluded road not far from interstate I 95 where the young couple was stripped of everything they had: but they were still wearing their jewelry. At some point, the young man attempted to confront their abductors when one of the criminals overreacted and shot him. The young girl, without hesitation, likely move toward her companion when the killer panicked and also quickly shot her. The two frightened killers, having lost control of the situation, did not bother with the jewelry and simply took the easiest spoils and drove off hastily. Since the killing occurred shortly after midnight, they were hundreds of miles away and in another state before their bodies were discovered.

If you have any information about this case, which you feel might be helpful, call Sumter County Sheriff's Office at 803-436-2017.

Recommended Reading

Lucas-Poncet, Sharyn. "The Mystery Couple," On online article by. Crime Library.

They Once Were Lost, but Now Are Found

We've finished our stories of mysterious disappearances, but in the course of our research we came across a number of fascinating and bizarre stories of people who vanished—but were found again. We include these as a bonus coda.

Runaway Mom

On February 8, 2002, Brenda Heist dropped off her eight year old daughter and twelve year old son at school in Lititz, Pennsylvania. At the time Brenda was going through an amicable divorce, but was despondent with her life in general.

Her company car was found several days later about 30 miles away in the city of York. The keys were not in the car and there was no indication that anything was wrong with the vehicle. Brenda vanished without a trace. She was declared legally dead in 2010 and her husband, Lee, who had remarried had also collected her life insurance policy.

Did Brenda walk away from her children, her marriage and her job, because she was downhearted? Or was it something else? How suspicious should we be of a husband who got both a divorce and her insurance money?

Eleven Years Later

After eleven years, there was little to hold out any hope that Brenda was still alive. But April 26, 2013 brought a great surprise. After more than a decade of living a double life as a vagrant, Brenda turned herself in to the sheriff's office in Monroe County in Key Largo, Florida, telling them that she was a missing person. Brenda said that she survived by hustling for food, panhandling and living under bridges all that time.

The police soon learned, however, that she was not completely truthful. Brenda had used various aliases over the years and also had been in trouble with the law. Furthermore, she had never contacted her family during those 11 long years.

On February 15, several months before turning herself in, Brenda was arrested for stealing a driver's license from a woman who had employed her to clean her house and then using her ID during a traffic stop. She was sentenced to serve two months in jail for that offense.

Then two days after serving time for that conviction, she turned herself in to the police stating that she was Brenda Heist who went missing for over a decade. The authorities also learned that she was wanted for a parole violation on other charges.

According to Lititz Detective John Schofield, who flew down to Florida to interview her, " She explained to me that she just snapped. She turned her back on her family, she turned her back on her friends, her co-workers. She said she thought of her family and her children every day, and her parents. However, she never acted on that and never made any phone calls—not one."

Brenda told police that she finally decided to turn herself in since she was at the end of her rope and also having health problems. She also said that she plans to go to Texas and live with her Mom. ("Missing mother who abandoned her two children, fled to Florida for 11 years and was declared illegally dead sentenced to one year in jail on a probation violation," Daily Mail Reporter. Online article, June 12, 2013. MailOnline.)

In May, Dr. Phil interviewed Brenda on the TV Today Show. He said, "You go from being a mom in suburbia with two kids and a husband at 11 that morning, to hitchhiking to Florida and staying in homeless camps along the way. Did you think or wonder that the children would be hurt by your going?" "Not at the time, I didn't," Brenda said. "But I knew that they would be hurt. But I just felt that there was no turning back." She asked her family to forgive her and then weakly attempted to justify her disappearance. ("A Dr. Phil interview: Runaway Mom Speaks Out," Online article, May 20, 2013, Dr. Phil.)

Brenda's son, Lee, who graduated from West Chester University plans to pursue a career in law enforcement. Her daughter, Morgan, is a sophomore at the same university. Her husband and two children were brokenhearted to learn that she willfully chose to live a secret vagrant life without them. They have also chosen not to be associated with her in any way. Who could blame them?

A Santa Rosa County Judge sentenced Brenda Heist (alias Kelsie Smith) at age 54, to one year in jail for violating probation resulting from her February arrest.

Brenda just walked away from her family and never looked back. She gave up everything to live a decadent life as a homeless person for over a decade. There are many questions, and they are all "Whys?". But there are no good answers.

We have sometimes thought of this when writing this book. Even when we are convinced that the missing person we're discussing was murdered, Brenda Heist shows that there is always another possibility.

Walled In

JoAnn Nichols, a 55-year-old popular elementary teacher, taught her last class on December 20, 1985. The following day she had a hair appointment but did not show up. JoAnn went missing for over 27 years.

Did she choose to disappear? If so, why? Was she murdered? If so, who did it?

JoAnn was 5-foot 7 and weighed 140 pounds with blond hair and blue eyes. She grew up on a farm in Northern Louisiana. While in graduate school at the University of Mississippi, she met and married James Nichols who taught at the university. James, whose father was a medical doctor, went to work for IBM and was then transferred to Poughkeepsie, New York.

James told the police that the last time he saw his wife was on December 21, when he went to work at IBM that morning. When the police arrived at the Nichols home after JoAnn disappeared, her car was also missing. Later on when the police returned, they noticed that her car was now in the driveway. James told the police that he found his wife's car locked at a nearby shopping center and drove it home. Poughkeepsie Detective Lieutenant Charles Mittelstaedt said that when he inspected the car, he found that it had been washed and vacuumed.

Later the police found a note on the Nichol's home computer, which indicated that JoAnn was depressed, but that she was not suicidal. Mittelstaedt said, "[James] sat across from me in my office, looked me straight in the face, and told us that he thought she was depressed, he hinted at maybe suicidal." Some speculated that she might have been despondent over the drowning death in 1982 of their 25-year-old son and only child.

James told a Poughkeepsie Journal reporter that his wife called on Christmas Eve and said that she was fine, but hung up when he asked where she was. Lt. Mittelstaedt said that James described the phone call differently, saying that his wife, who was very religious, had a new name, made peace with God and not to try to find her.

When James was placed under surveillance, they found out that he was visiting another woman just several weeks after his wife disappeared. When they approached James about his behavior, he replied, "If you don't have a warrant for my arrest, you can talk to my lawyer," according to Mittelstaedt. It was the last time the police spoke to him.

Several detectives were assigned to the case full time, but they were unable to find any clues or leads to JoAnn's whereabouts or evidence that there was foul play, so James was never arrested. The police didn't have a body or a weapon. Furthermore, investigators never searched the house, because they did not have legal grounds to obtain a warrant. ("Cop in NY remains case always suspected husband," Michael Hill. Online article, July 3, 2013.)

The Evil that Men Do—Can Sometimes be Found After They Die

In December 2012, James died of natural causes at the age of 82. He was found slumped in a chair inside his cluttered house. He was a loner who withdrew from his neighbors and lived a "hermit-like" life in his small white house all those years.

There were no relatives to claim his body, so a contractor was hired to clean out his house. He had a major job on his hands since James was known to be a hoarder and the house was filled with junk. When the contractor worked his way down to the basement and started to clean out all the debris, he discovered a false wall. Behind the wall he found a sealed plastic container about the size of an ordinary garbage can. When he opened the container, he found a large black garbage bag tied with a thin rope. When he untied the bag, he was shocked to discover the skeletal remains of a human being.

Who was the skeleton in the sealed bag? And who stuffed someone in that container?

The cleaning was halted momentarily since the contractor needed a break, and the authorities were notified. Duchess County Medical Examiner Dr. Karl Reiber identified the decayed bones as JoAnn Nichols. Reiber stated that a positive identification was made on the basis of her dental records. He also said that JoAnn died as a result of a blunt-force trauma to her head.

When the medical examiner released the startling information to the public, detectives on the case said they suspected that her husband had killed her. James, however, was never publicly named as a suspect, which was surprising.

Mittelstaedt, now retired, said, "I remember the case like it happened yesterday because every time I drove past her house, I wondered if she was in there. It's a sin that he got away with it all these years. I probably shouldn't say this because it's not politically correct but I hope he rots in hell."

It is incomprehensible how James could live with all that trash he collected for almost thirty years with his wife "walled" only a short distance away. JoAnn was a beloved teacher and well-liked by everyone, well, almost everyone.

So ended a long mystery. By the way, we feel that James was guilty as sin and also hope that he's rotting in hell.

He's Gone—He's Gone

On May 31, 2010, Ervin Robinson, age 52, dropped out of sight from his home in Pelican Bay, Texas. His wife Neola, however, told the police that her husband left with another woman. The authorities were suspicious and felt that Neola knew more than she was telling them. But what did Neola know?

Two weeks before his disappearance, Robinson transferred money from their joint checking account and opened a checking account in his name only. Several days later, the police were called to the Robinson residence to deal with a domestic dispute. Neola had locked her husband outside because he refused to give her some money. Later that evening, Neola went to a bar where she told a friend that she was going to murder her husband. Was she just angry and started talking bravely after a few drinks?

Two days before Robinson's disappearance, he was seen on a store security video about 20 miles from his home purchasing food and some mattresses. Was that activity related to his disappearance?

The Robinsons', who had been married for three years, had more than their share of marital problems. They both also had a shady past. A criminal background check revealed that Robinson had a number of arrests including theft, burglary and several DWIs. Neola, on the other hand, was known to have used multiple surnames.

Neighbors told the police that the Robinsons' could often be heard arguing and that they also had violent episodes. One of Robinson's friends told the police that Neola was jealous of his female companions. Neola said to one of her husband's friends that if he came home "he's going to be missing some body parts, or I'm going to kill him and I don't care if I go to prison." Neither option seemed to bode well for Robinson.

Some of Robinson's friends said he would not have gone off and left without saying goodbye. Others who knew him said he was a passionate biker and it was very strange that he left his Harley, his prize possession, behind.

In early June, Neola went to his work place, the T J Machine & tool company, and cried out, "He's gone. He's gone." Robinson's work supervisor Michael Wright said that he was a reliable employee and would have told him if he was planning on leaving. He then went on to say that he wondered why Robinson did not pick up his paycheck. Wright also proceeded to file a missing person's report when Robinson continued not to show up for work.

When the police searched the Robinson home sometime in June, they found what appeared to be a large bloodstain in the bathroom. One of the officers commented on how clean the house was compared to an earlier visit when they responded to a domestic dispute when it was dirty and cluttered. ("Texas woman's husband who disappeared three years ago found buried in her yard," Online article, July 17, 2013. Fox News.)

Did Neola suddenly acquire the virtue of neatness or was there a more ominous explanation?

Living with Murder

For three years, Neola was steadfast—she stuck to her story. But in July 2013, Texas Rangers who were called in early to help the police got a tip suggesting that they search the Robinson property. After carefully going over the home and its surroundings, they were shocked to find what they were looking for.

Neola's husband had not gone very far, after all. He showed up in the most outlandish place. The Rangers dug up Robinson's buried body—not in the basement, not in the backyard, but of all places--in the very conspicuous front yard.

What really happened? Did Neola murder her husband and then bury him all by herself? And why did she choose such an exposed place?

In mid-July, after being confronted with the recently dug up evidence, Neola decided to confess. She said that when her husband grabbed her arm during a quarrel, she sprayed his eyes with a chemical and then stabbed him in the hand with a knife. Neola continued on saying that her husband went to sleep in a chair in the living room and she retired to the bedroom.

The next morning Neola said that she found her husband dead in the chair. Then late that night, Neola told the authorities that she placed him on an air mattress and buried him in a hole on the front lawn that had been dug earlier for a water line that had ben repaired. The police felt that the burial spot was the same place where Neola had told them she buried a dog. ("Affidavit: Wife says she stabbed husband, found him dead next morning," Marjorie Owens. Online article, WFAA.com Dallas | Fort Worth.)

Neola was charged with the murder of her husband and was placed in the Tarrant County jail with bail set at $150,000. She is on suicide watch and also awaiting a complete mental health evaluation.

She did, however, kill her husband and bury him just a few feet from her front door. What was Neola thinking as she walked by, and daily looked at that irregular rectangular plot of dirt—with its buried secret?

Six Skeletons

On September 17, 2013, several Oklahoma Highway Patrol troopers were training with new underwater sonar equipment on Foss Lake in Custer County, Oklahoma. The murky water in the lake only allowed a visibility of six to twelve inches. Trooper diver Darrell Splawn said, "The visibility was only four inches at the bottom. You can't see anything, you basically just go down there and feel with your hands. It's just a blind feel."

Trooper George Hoyle went about 50 feet out on the lake from the end of a boat ramp to begin checking out the new sonar equipment. The depth of the silt-laden lake at that point was only 12 feet. The lake level, however, was about 13 feet below normal due to a drought.

Hoyle did not expect to find anything. After all, it was a routine training assignment and he was just testing out a new scanner. He was surprised, however, when he picked up a good image of two cars close to each other on the bottom of the lake. The general consensus was that the cars had been stolen and dumped into the lake some time ago and that was that. But how did the cars get out that far in the lake?

The next day, when they pulled the two vehicles out of the water, they were shocked to learn that they made an extraordinary discovery. The two submerged cars contained bones in each of them. But who were the skeletal remains? And what happened?

While it wasn't supposed to be, an ordinary training mission had possibly turned into a cold case mystery—and maybe even solving one or two. ("Oklahoma lake bodies: Diver, trooper recount discovery," Ed Payne, Michael Martinez and Ed Lavandera. Online article, CNN, September 19, 2013.)

The Blue Camaro

They pulled up 1969 blue Chevrolet Camaro first. When the police got their initial look at the rusted and corroded Camaro, they noticed that all four windows were rolled down. When the police searched the car, they found two rifles and also alcohol containers inside the vehicle.

The big mystery, however, was to determine the identity of the remains. The medical examiner concluded that the driver of the Camaro was a male teenager, while the two teenagers in the rear seat were a female and a male. The examiner's findings matched the type of vehicle, gender and ages of the teenagers from Sayre, Oklahoma who disappeared on November 20, 1970 over four decades ago. The owner of the Camaro Jimmy Williams, 16, from Sayre, drove the car, while Thomas Rios and Leah Johnson, both 18, were passengers.

When Trooper Hoyle examined the car, he said that it appeared the driver changed to a lower gear as it went into the water. Gary Williams, who still resides in Sayre, was Jimmy's younger brother and age 12 at the time of the disappearance, was given permission to examine the Camaro. Gary stated that the car was in neutral and not in the first gear when he looked it over. Gary said that he took pictures, but when he showed the photos to the mechanic, he declined to comment on the matter.

The police were curious why the two cars were faced in different directions and close to each other on the bottom of the lake. The Camaro appeared to be facing in the wrong direction. How did the cars enter the lake and end up that way?

Gary said that since the Camaro had been turned around, it appeared to have entered the lake backwards. Gary seems to be suggesting that the car was in neutral and went into the water backwards because someone had already killed its occupants and was disposing of the evidence this way. But Hoyle thought that the driver of the Camaro might have tried to turn the car in an attempt to stop from going into the lake and also pointed out that damage to the undercarriage of the Camaro indicated that it had been in an accident. The car's gear might also have been shifted during the impact with the water and any struggle to get out.

On that fateful night, some 43 years ago, the three teenagers were supposed to go to a football game, but they were never seen again. We wondered if their radio was tuned to the station where they were listening to

Loretta Lynn singing "Coal Miner's Daughter", one of the top country hit songs of the year. Whatever they were listening to, the car's radio remained tuned to the same station for the next 43 years.

There were various suggestions made at the time of their disappearance about what might have happened to the three teenagers. Some thought they might have run off to California, others thought that foul play might have been involved, but every lead just went nowhere.

DNA samples have been collected from all of the families and sent to the University of North Texas Health Science Center for testing. We feel it's most likely that the results from the DNA reference laboratory will eventually confirm the identities and findings of the medical examiner. Meanwhile a cold case committee has been appointed to review the case. Although it seems likely that the driver of the Camaro accidentally drove the car into the lake and the three youths drowned, the puzzling position of the car and the damage to it leaves some lingering mystery.

In any case, the discovery of the car ends the most significant part of the mystery for the families and, we hope, brings them some sense of peace and closure. ("Coroner: Remains from Oklahoma lake math genders, ages of six missing people," Michael Martinez. Online article, CNN, October 13, 2013.)

The Green Chevrolet

When the second car, the 1952 Green Chevrolet, was pulled out from the lake, they noticed that the driver's side door was wide open. Later, when the police searched the car they found alcohol containers inside the vehicle. The most important finding, however, was the astonishing discovery that the vehicle contained the skeletal remains of three people.

The medical examiner concluded that the remains belonged to an older man, an adult male and an adult female. The findings matched the disappearance of John Alva Porter, 69, Cleburn Hammack, 42, and Nora Marie Duncan, 58, when they went missing in their 1952 Chevrolet on April 8, 1969 over four decades ago.

The three adults were apparently last seen when someone was giving them a push to get their car started. At the time it was generally thought that they were the victims of foul play. The authorities, however, were never able to find any evidence to support that theory.

Debbie McNanamon was 13 years old when her grandfather John Porter disappeared in a green 1952 Chevrolet in the spring of 1969. She has agonized all these years since he vanished. Debbie said that she often took her children and grandchildren to the lake to swim and also to feed the fish and ducks.

"As the years rolled by—we're not too far from the lake, maybe 20 miles—we'd think, Yeah, I think he's in the lake. It's a terrible thing to know that they were there for 44 years," she said. ("Oklahoma Sunken Cars: Mysteries Solved for Families With Vanished Relatives," Christina Ng. Online article, ABC NEWS, September 20, 2013.)

DNA samples have been collected from family members and sent to a DNA reference laboratory. We feel it is most likely that the results will match the tentative findings of the medical examiner. Meanwhile, the authorities have appointed a committee to review the cold case. But it seems likely that the driver of the car, however, accidentally drove into the lake and the three adults drowned.

We feel the results will be the resolution of a very cold case.

How to Escape from a Submerged Car

Over 400 people die each year from being submerged in an automobile. While any car accident is frightening, being trapped inside a car under water is terrifying. Most deaths, however, are due to panic and not having an understanding of what to do.

The important thing is to remain calm. While you don't have much time, you can save your life and others if you have a planned procedure of what to do. Just one example of what not to do—don't use your cell phone.

Since no one-survival plan fits all, we recommend that you search the Internet. There are number of excellent sites, which can help you prepare a safe escape procedure that suits you best. In general, however, the best advice seems to be to act quickly and to try to get out through the window. Once the car has started sinking, it's very difficult to open the door until the pressure has equalized.

Gone, but Not Very Far

In January 1984, Joseph Schexnider, 22, was scheduled to appear in court for possession of a stolen vehicle, but he never showed up. When the police went to his home to take him into custody, they found that he was gone. Schexnider not only ran away from the law, but he went missing for 27 years. Unbelievably, however, he never left his hometown of Abbeville, in southwestern Louisiana. But--where was he?

Those who knew Schexnider described him as a nice guy and relaxed, but someone who marched to his own drumbeat. He ran off from home when he was only nine or ten years of age. Several years later, he decided to leave high school in the ninth grade.

While he took odd jobs, he quickly moved on from one job to another. He served briefly in the Louisiana National Guard and left with a medical discharge. His brother, Robert, said, "He told me he'd seen every state in the country." He followed carnivals and even joined a circus for a while. Schexnider was a young man who was prone to wander from an early age.

His family never reported him missing over all those years, and no one ever searched for him. While his mother worried about him, his family felt that he always had an irresistible impulse to travel and assumed that he was doing what he wanted to do.

A Dead End

In May 2011, about three decades after he disappeared, construction workers made a startling discovery. While doing renovations on the second floor of the Abbeville National Bank in Louisiana, they found some bones and clothing inside a fireplace. When they looked more closely, the rest of the body was hung up in the interior of the fireplace and lodged in the brick chimney.

The body was decomposed and the skeleton was just hung together by the victim's clothing. Investigators found a long yellow sleeve shirt, a pair of jeans, tennis shoes, gloves and jockey shorts with the name Joseph Schexnider printed on the waistband. They also found his wallet, which contained his birth certificate and a social security card. ("Funeral for man entombed for 27 years in chimney," Mary Foster. Online article, August 12, 2011, Yahoo News.)

"This was absolutely the first chimney recovery we had ever had," said Mary Manhein, director of Forensic Anthropology and Computer Enhancement Services (FACES), the laboratory at Louisiana State University that identified Schexnider's bones and provided the DNA testing confirming that the remains were those of Joseph Schexnider. ("Skeleton Found in Chimney 27 years After Man Disappeared," Christina Caron. Online article, July 27, 2011, ABCNEWS.)

Lt. David Hardy chief of investigations for the Abbeville Police Department said, "From the way the skeleton was recovered, it appeared Schexnider went into the 14-inch-by-14-inch chimney feet first. Because the chimney narrowed sharply at the bottom, he then was apparently unable to maneuver his way back out."

But why did he end up inside the chimney? Was it an attempt to rob the bank, an accident, just hiding or something more sinister?

Since Schexnider was trapped in the brick chimney of the Abbeville bank, many thought that he planned to rob the bank. The police did not find any burglary tools or any kind of a bag to carry off the money, which he most likely would have had if he planned to commit a robbery.

While Schexnider didn't always think out things clearly and thoroughly, it's puzzling why he would have entered such a narrow chimney even though he had a lean and lanky build. But apparently, he didn't know that the chimney tapered on its way down and ended with only a narrow opening to the fireplace on the second floor. Nevertheless, it's still possible, but not too likely that it was a misconceived burglary by Schexnider.

Access to the roof of the bank building was not that difficult. Jason Herbert said that when he was a kid he also climbed up there, and now that he's a detective with the Abbeville Police he has chased kids off the rooftops. In 1987 when workmen capped off the chimney, they were unaware that Schexnider had been trapped in that defunct smokestack for three years. ("Funeral for man entombed for 27 years in chimney," Mary Foster. Online article, August 12, 2011, Yahoo News.)

We wondered how the workmen felt when they learned that they had accidentally dropped small amounts of concrete and debris down on poor Schexnider's skeletal remains?

There is no way to know if Schexnider called out for help when he found himself stuck in the chimney. He was above the second floor, encased in bricks and it's most likely his cries for help could not be heard down on the street. Furthermore, the second floor of the bank was used for storage for years and it was seldom that anyone ever went up there. A cell phone might have saved his life, but they were not widely available at the time he went missing.

Manhein felt that Schexnider probably died within a few days after entering the chimney, but there was no way to determine how he died. She went on to say that there were no indications of foul play since his bones did not show any signs of trauma. The police speculated that he died of dehydration and starvation.

It's possible that when Schexnider ran from the law that he decided to climb up on top of the bank roof and hide, which he likely often did as a kid. He was frightened and without thinking, he quickly entered the chimney. He probably felt that he could slide down the chimney and crawl out at the bottom onto the second floor. But sadly, he got stuck on his way downward and couldn't go up or down—and he died there.

We think the following scenario is more likely. He did chose to access the roof of the bank, because he wanted to avoid the police. In looking around for a place to hide, he decided to quickly take cover in the chimney.

He then entered the chimney and positioned himself a short distance from the top as a temporary hiding place. He planned on exiting when he felt it was safe to come out.

It was, however, a precarious place to hide because there was no way for him to secure himself there for some time. After a while, he likely became weary and lost control of where he was positioned and accidentally fell down lower in the chimney and got trapped—and entombed for the next 27 years. We're just grateful this never happened to Santa.

Two Who Vanished

On May 29, 1971, Cheryl Miller and Pam Jackson, both 17, were driving at night on a lonely rural road headed out to an end-of-the-school-year party. Since they weren't sure of the directions, they decided to follow several young male classmates in their car who were also on their way to the get-together. It was a delightful, warm Saturday night: school was over and the two happy teenagers were looking forward to celebrating with their schoolmates at the gravel pit, which was about 15 miles from Vermillion. South Dakota.

In the year of their disappearance, 500,000 people marched to Washington, D.C. in protest to the Vietnam War. National Public Radio began programming. The voting age was lowered from 21 to 18. The Rolling Stones released the politically incorrect but wonderful, "Brown Sugar." And D.B. Cooper parachuted from a Northwest Orient Airlines plane he hijacked with $200,000 (equivalent to $1.17 million in 2014). He was never seen or heard from again.

As Sheryl and Pam were hurriedly following along in the 1960 beige Studebaker Lark, they lost site of their schoolmates. It was not too surprising, since visibility is poor at night driving on narrow and windy country roads. Just when they were close to their destination, something terrible happened: all of a sudden, it occurred in a moment, in the blink of an eye.

Sheryl and Pam never made it to the party, and they never made it back home. They just seemed to vanish. No one knows what happened.

Background

In the spring of 1971, Sheryl Miller, a junior in high school, was living with her grandfather who lived in Vermillion. Sheryl's close friend, Pam Stewart, described Sheryl thusly: "She was a smart girl, and she learned to be independent. She was focused. She knew right, she knew wrong, and she knew what she wanted and what she didn't want."

Sheryl has a part-time job at a hospital in Vermillion, which allowed her to be close to her grandmother who was dying of cancer. She also attended to her elderly grandfather.

Sheryl always wanted to go into fashion design. She was very neat and enjoyed dressing and looking her best. She and Stewart had planned to tour California after they graduated.

Pam Jackson, who also was a junior in high school and Sheryl's friend, was reared on a farm in the small town of Alcester, South Dakota. She was the youngest of four children and grew up with pet cats, dogs and other small animals. Pam enjoyed singing in the high school chorus and also participated in 4-H arts and crafts. She also worked part-time at the hospital at Vermillion. Pam enjoyed sewing and had a passion for dressmaking.

Sheryl and Pam had plans for careers and what they wanted to do. But what they didn't have--was time to live.

The Night They Disappeared

On that pleasant Saturday morning, Sheryl Miller and Pam Stewart wanted to take Sheryl's grandfather's good car to go the party that night. They washed and vacuumed the car hoping to convince him to use it, but he refused. Instead, they agreed to take the grandfather's older 1960 Studebaker. Later that day, Stewart got a phone call asking her to babysit for the evening. She decided to forego the party and took the babysitting job.

Meanwhile, that afternoon Pam Jackson was sewing a dress for a school function. Early that evening, Pam asked her mother if she could attend the classmates party with Cheryl. At first her mother said no, but then said it was all right to go.

That evening Sheryl and Pam visited Sheryl's grandmother in the hospital. After leaving the hospital around 9:30 p.m., they met up with several young lads who were classmates and also on the way to the party. The two young ladies then followed their classmates for a while, but then somewhere along the way lost track of their car. Sheryl and Pam never made it to the party.

Very early Sunday morning, Adele Jackson wondered why her daughter had not turned out the kitchen light, which she was supposed to do when she returned home. When Adele looked into Pam's bedroom, she was surprised to see that she wasn't there. She wondered where she could be.

Somewhere on their way to the gravel pit, Sheryl and Pam went missing along with the 1960 Studebaker. For over 40 heartbreaking years, both families and friends wondered where they were.

The Investigation

When the authorities questioned the young male schoolmates, they said that after their meeting with Cheryl and Pam that the two young women decided to follow them in their car to the party. At one point the boys inadvertently drove past the turn to the gravel pit, but when the drove back they lost track of Cheryl and Pam. They proceeded to drive on to the party: when they looked back in their rear view mirror, their two classmates were nowhere in sight.

Law enforcement officials, as well as family members and friends searched the area countless times, but no trace of Cheryl or Pam or their car was ever found. The authorities speculated that the teenagers took the wrong road while driving in the dark and plunged into the Missouri River, which flowed between the South Dakota and Nebraska border.

Furthermore, they felt that the car would have sunk to the bottom quickly in the strong current, and then got covered over with sand in just a few hours. Officials maintained that locating the car in the treacherous current would have been very difficult, and diving was futile due to poor visibility. Consequently, they decided not to drag the river. This seems to us to be a weak excuse for sloppy work.

There were theories that drug dealers, beatniks and counter-culture groups who were living in the outlying areas of Vermillion might have abducted the two young women. Eventually, it turned out that there was no evidence to support that theory.

The authorities prevailing theory was that the couple just ran off together. The two teenagers, however, had jobs and had been paid that day, but did not take their paychecks with them. They did not pack any clothing or take other personal items along. Furthermore, there was no evidence that they had been drinking. They were well thought of and simply not the type to just run off and leave everything behind.

It appeared more likely that the teenagers apparently just headed off to attend a fun party with other classmates. But, somehow they went missing. What happened? Where were they?

Several years later, investigators checked out Henry Lucas, a serial killer, who stated that he had killed several people in South Dakota. It turned out that this theory was unfounded and the investigation led nowhere. These kinds of statements by known murderers can't simply be ignored and must be followed up, but often take up an inordinate amount of time. ("Families of missing girls yearn for closure," Steve Young. Online article, November 7, 2006.)

The case of the two South Dakota teenagers went cold and stayed cold.

A Prime Suspect

[David] Lykken was convicted in November 1990 of kidnapping and sexually assaulting a former girlfriend. At his sentence hearing the following February, five women with whom Lykken had been romantically involved between 1977 and 1990 testified that he would beat them and threaten to kill them. Several said he sexually assaulted them. Because Lykken also was convicted in Minnehaha County in 1983 for felony burglary stemming from the home invasion, kidnapping and assault of one former girlfriend, Clay County Circuit Judge E.W. Hertz was able to sentence him as a habitual offender. ("Pamela Jackson/Cheryl Miller, 1971, South Dakota – Cold Case Investigations, Online article, November 7, 2006." "Bones found in farm search," September 9, 2004.)

In 1991, Judge Hertz gave Lykken a 227-year sentence in the South Dakota State Penitentiary for rape and kidnapping.

At the time of the 1990 case, state attorney Craig Thompson suggested the possibility that Lykken, who was a classmate of Sheryl and Pam, might have been involved in their disappearance. The authorities, however, did not have sufficient evidence to move forward on the case. The investigation into the disappearance of Sheryl and Pam in 1971 went cold again.

Case Reopened

No trace of the two teenagers disappearance ever surfaced and the case faded until 2004 when investigators in the South Dakota Division of Criminal Investigations Cold Case Unit reopened the case. In September of that year, a warrant was issued authorizing the authorities to search the Lykken's farm, which was David Lykken's home as a teenager in 1971, and was less than two miles from the gravel pit where the teenagers were headed the evening they disappeared.

Lykken, age 50, and incarcerated for life, was now a suspect again in the disappearance of Sheryl and Pam 33 years ago. (And, we think, an excellent suspect!) Chris followed the case on WebSleuths.com before it was solved and thought Lykken was probably guilty. Investigators proceeded to conduct a thorough search of the farm. They could not afford to overlook anything, no matter how insignificant, since modern technological techniques were now available to them that were not know decades earlier.

The search team found bones (unrelated to the crime), clothing, a purse, photographs, newspaper articles and a variety of other items—but no red Studebaker. The authorities did not elaborate on their findings.

In 2007, A Union County grand jury then indicted Lykken on two counts of premeditated murder, two counts of felon murder and two counts of murder in the disappearance of Sheryl and Pam. He was charged in part on evidence obtained from an audio tape recording made in jail

The jailhouse tape was made secretly by Aloysius Black Crow, who recorded a conversation between himself and another inmate who pretended he was Lykken confessing to the murders of Sheryl and Pam. The following year, Crow pleaded guilty to two counts of perjury when he lied about Lykken admitting to causing the death of the two teenagers. Attorney General Larry Long dropped the case when he learned that the jailhouse informant, Crow, faked the tape-recorded confession. ("South Dakota girls missing since 1971 killed in car crash, officials say," Online article, Associated Press, April 16, 2014.)

Simply Serendipity

In 2013, South Dakota was suffering from a severe drought. In September of that year, a fisherman from the area who was familiar with the case noticed the wheels of a car protruding out of Brule Creek. The turned-over car was located under a bridge and close to the gravel pit near Elk Point about 15 miles from Vermillion.

The car started to fall apart when the wrecking crew attempted to lift it up from the creek: they ended up eventually by retrieving the vehicle in several sections. The authorities found the remains of two humans in the front seat. The car was in high gear and the switch on the dashboard showed that the headlights were turned on when the car entered the water.

A wristwatch, with its strap still intact, showed that the watch stopped at 10:20 p.m.

Investigators showed photographs of the two bodies with their clothing still well preserved along with Cheryl Miller's purse, and also her driver's license showing her pretty smiling face. Pam Jackson did not have her purse with her.

Attorney Marty Jackley confirmed that the personal items and DNA testing made a positive identification that the remains were those of the missing teenagers. Jackley said, "It's consistent with a car accident. To start with, the forensic pathology and anthropology reports indicate that there's no type of injury that would be consistent with or caused by foul play or inappropriate conduct." He also pointed out that there was no way to determine whether a tire blowout was responsible for the crash, but that the tread on the one damaged tire was worn thin. ("South Dakota girls missing since 1971 killed in car crash, officials say," Online article, Associated Press, April 16, 2014.)

What We Think Happened

Cheryl and Pam were two spirited well-meaning teenagers out to enjoy a party with other high school classmates at the end of the school year. It's something most of us have done during those carefree days of youth.

Early that Saturday evening, after Sheryl got permission to take her grandfather's old Studebaker, she picked up her friend Pam. They took time to visit Cheryl's grandmother in the hospital that unlucky night before leaving around 9:30 p. m. for the high school get-together.

Since they were unsure of the directions to the gravel pit near Elk Point some 15 miles away, they decided to follow three male classmates who were also going to the party. Several days later, however, LuAnn Scrensen-Denke, a close friend and classmate, said, "Pam knew the roads really well."

Unfortunately, many high school youngsters take unnecessary risks, and it's likely the two teenagers were driving faster than they should to keep up with their classmates. Furthermore, night driving on unfamiliar roads in a rural area can be deceptively hazardous. At some point, the two girls lost track of their schoolmates' car.

We think that when they were just less than a mile from the gravel pit and likely traveling at an excessive speed that they had a tire blowout. The Studebaker quickly went out of control, turned over and plunged into Brule Creek. It was found upside down beneath a small bridge in the creek.

Even if two people are trapped in an upright vehicle under water in daylight hours, and reasonably aware of the situation, they only have a very short time to escape safely.

The teenager's accident happened shockingly fast: they most likely were stunned, and perhaps rendered unconscious. They were upside down in the creek, and in that dazed condition they didn't have time to think or orient themselves in the dark. We also think that it's likely the two teenagers never knew what happened.

If they had lived out their normal life, Cheryl and Pam would most likely have had grandchildren the same age as they were, when they vanished that dark Saturday night.

Flack from the Farm Search

In 2014, Sioux Falls Attorney Mike Butler, who represented David Lykken said that the state has never apologized to his family for searching the farm, along with allegations that turned out to be false. "This whole thing with a man being charged, the Lykken family farm being plowed under," Butler said of the search. "That family suffered needlessly for a long time."

David Lykken's brother, Kerwyn, spokesperson for the family, felt that they were owed an apology. The Lykken family filed a $400,000 lawsuit arguing that the authorities caused significant property damage during the searches and falsely accused the family of not cooperating.

Jackley pointed out that the two federal courts upheld the manner in which the search was done. "With that said, it's unfortunate that when we are searching and trying to help families that we disrupt things, that we affect lives," he said. "That search was done legally and with the full intention of trying to help the family of a community find the two missing 17-year-olds."

The Families

Families always want to know what happened when loved ones vanish in the blink of a moment and are never heard from again.

The families of Sheryl and Pam finally have closure, as well as the peace of mind knowing that they died quickly at the time of the accident rather than suffering through some horrendous torture or subjugation.

Jackley read a statement from them: "Our day has come through this journey for answers pertaining to our sister Sherry [sic] and dear friend Pam, for we will be able to finish the last chapter of this journey." ("South Dakota girls missing since 1971 killed in car crash, officials say," Online article, Associated Press, April 16, 2014.)

In all our stories, we've given you our best ideas as to what happened. We hope that some of them are eventually resolved, but honestly think that this might only occur in, at most, one or two cases. But as the stories in the coda show, life can be very surprising. All of our mysteries carry a question mark.

Bibliography

Introduction

Missing Persons and Unidentified Persons Statistics 2012, Online article.

The District Attorney Goes Missing

"AG Corbett & Centre County DA Gricar announce breakup of $1.5 million heroin & cocaine organization." Online article, Pennsylvania Office of Attorney General, March 31, 2005.

Bock, Greg. "Bellefonte chief doubts Hells Angels Gricar story," Online article, *Altoona Mirror*, September 22, 2013.

"Cops no closer to finding DA." Online article, PhillyTrib.com | *The Philadelphia Tribune*, January 15, 2012.

James, Sara. "Missing District Attorney," Online article, May 15, 2006.

JJinPhila. "Revisiting the Laptop, the Drive, and the Case," Online article, CentreDaily.com, July 12, 2009.

_____. "The Least Weak Evidence for Suicide," Online article, CentreDaily.com, September 13, 2010.

_____. "The Least Weak Evidence for Walkaway," Online article, CentreDaily.com, November 19, 2010.

"Ray Gricar's disappearance likely not linked to Jerry Sandusky case, investigators say." Online article, November 11, 2011.

"Ray Gricar mystery: DA's privacy adds to intrigue surrounding his disappearance," Sara Ganim. Online article, *The Patriot-News,* April 15, 2012).

Ray Gricar – Wikipedia, the free encyclopedia.

Timeline—Ray Gricar. Online article, March 31, 2010.

The Last Midnight Ride

Adams, Helen Colwell "The Curious Case of Jonathan Luna," Online article, Updated October 2, 2008.

CentreDaily.com Jonathan Luna jjinPhila. Of Theories December 2009. CentreDailyTimes.

Jonathan Luna – Wikipedia, the free encyclopedia.

Keisling, William. *The Midnight ride of Jonathan Luna,* Harrisburg, PA. Yardbird Books, 2004 – 2008.

The Doctor Disappears the Day the Buildings Came Tumbling Down

Fass, Mark. "Last Seen On September 10th," Online article, *New York Magazine,* June 26, 2006.

"Sneha Anne Phillips," Wikipedia, the free encyclopedia.

Bonnie and Mitchel: Long Time Gone, Gone

Bickwit, Bonita. Online article, July 27, 1973 (Porchlight International for the Missing & Unidentified).

Greenberg, Eric J. "Without A TRACE: Without A TRACE," Online article, The Jewish Week, July 24, 1998.

Glamour Girl Gone

"Jean Spangler." Disappearance Timeline Theories & Suspects. Online article.

"Jean Spangler" – Wikipedia- the free encyclopedia.

Rasmussen, Ceilia. "Mystery of Missing Starlet Was Never Solved," Online article, *Los Angeles Times*, October 20, 2002.

USS Dorado (SS - 248) On Eternal Patrol

Campbell, Douglas E.*USS Dorado (SS-248): On Eternal Patrol,* lulu.com, 2011.

Howard, Ed. "Subsowespac.org. Pacific War Book Review," Online article, Updated March 22, 2013."

_____. "Subsowespac.org. USS Dorado (SS-248)," Online article. Updated March 22, 2013.

Where Did Heinrich Go?

Heinrich Müller (Gestapo) – Wikipedia, the free encyclopedia.

Naftali, Timothy et al. "Analysis of the Name File of Heinrich Müller." Record Group 263: Records of the Central Intelligence Agency.

"Nazi Gestapo chief 'buried in Jewish cemetery,'" October 31, 2013. News Daily.

Rising, David. "Newly Discovered Heinrich Müller Death Certificate Indicates Nazi Head of Gestapo Died in Berlin (PHOTOS)" Online article, October 31, 2013

Did They or Didn't they?

Babyak, Jolene. *Breaking the Rock: The Great Escape from Alcatraz.* Berkeley, California, Ariel Vamp Press, 2001.

"June 1962 Alcatraz Escape," From Wikipedia, the free encyclopedia.

McFadden, Robert D. "Tale of 3 Inmates Who Vanished From Alcatraz Maintains Intrigue 50 Years Later." Online article, June 9, 2012, N.Y.Times.com.

Milton, Giles. "Escape From Alcatraz: The True Story," Online article, June 12, 2012.

The White Bird Disappears

Bak, Richard. *The Big Jump.* Hoboken, New Jersey. John Wiley & Sons, Inc. 2011.

Jackson, Joe. *Atlantic Fever.* New York, Picador. Farrar, Straus and Giroux, 2012.

Daniel, James. "Is this where the aviation pioneers who vanished while trying to beat Charles Lindbergh crashed? Frenchman identifies tiny island off the Canadian coast," Online article, MailOnline, June 29, 2013.

Woollaston, Victoria. "What happened to the *White Bird*? Fresh search for French plane that mysteriously disappeared as it tried to cross the Atlantic ten days before Charles Lindbergh's record breaking solo flight," Online article, MailOnline, May 10, 2013.

A Body Tumbled from the Sky

Norris, William. *The Man Who Fell From the Sky.* Haines City, Florida. SynergEBooks, 2000.

Milton, Giles. "High Jump: The Strange Death of Alfred Loewenstein, the World's Richest Man," Online article, April 30, 2013.

Stan. "The Strange Disappearance of Alfred Loewenstein," Online article, September 14, 2011.

"The Man Who Fell From the Sky," Online article, March 12, 2009. Thoughtcrime.

One Missing from the Long Gray Line

Maihafer, Harry J. *Oblivion: The Mystery of West Point Cadet Richard Cox.* Washington, D.C., Brassey's Inc. 1996.

Taylor, Troy. "The Devil's Right Hand: The Vanished Cadet," Online article, January 7, 2013.

An Unknown Civil Rights Pioneer

Elias, Robert. "Robert Elias: Lloyd Gaines, a lost hero of civil rights." The Cap Times, Online article, Copyright 2013.

"FBI Asked To Reopen Lloyd Gaines Case,." Associated Press. Diverse Issues in Higher Education. Online article, March 5, 2007.

Garrison, Chad. "The Mystery of Lloyd Gaines." - - News – St. Louis – Riverfront Times. Online article, April 4, 2007.

Greenberg, Ben, "Recy Talor may finally see Alabama acknowledge her 1944 rape." Online article, March 17, 2011. The Civil Rights Cold Case Project.

Kluger, Richard, *Simple Justice*. New York, Vintage Books, 1977.

Linder, Douglas. O. "Before Brown: Charles H. Houston and the Gaines Case." Online article 2000.

"Lloyd L. Gaines" - Wikipedia, the free encyclopedia. Online article.

Mitchell, Jerry. "Journey to Justice." Online article, November 22, 2010.

Found—but Still Lost

Parker-Lucas, Sharyn. "The Mystery Couple," On online article by. Crime Library, on truTV.com.

Wermers, Jason. "Couple Missing 1973 compared to 'Jacque and Jill' 1976 Sumter Co SC, Online article, August 26, 2009.

They Once Were Lost, but Now Are Found

Runaway Mom

"A Dr. Phil interview: Runaway Mom Speaks Out," Online article, May 20, 2013, Dr. Phil.

Knapp, Tom. "Brenda Heist, who disappeared from Lititz home 11 years ago, sentenced to year in jail," Online article, June 11, 2013, Lancaster Online.

"Missing mother who abandoned her two children, fled to Florida for 11 years and was declared illegally dead sentenced to one year in jail on a probation violation," Online article, June 12, 2013. MailOnline.

"Mom Brenda Heist resurfaces 11 years after abandoning kids," Online article, May 2, 2013, CBSNEWS.

Staffer, Cindy. "Brenda Heist back in Jail in Florida," Lancaster Online article, Updated May 4, 2013.

Walled In

Hill, Michael. "Cop in NY remains case always suspected husband," Online article, July 3, 2013.

Yee, Vivian. "In Cluttered Home, a Dark Secret 3 Decades Old," Online article, July 15, 2013,

He's Gone—He's Gone

Miller, Bill. "Body of Pelican Bay man missing for 3 years found in front yard," Online article, July 17, 2013, *Star-Telegram.*

Owens, Marjorie. "Affidavit: Wife says she stabbed husband, found him dead next morning," Online article, WFAA.com Dallas | Fort Worth.

Texas woman's husband who disappeared three years ago found buried in her yard," Online article, July 17, 2013. Fox News.

Six Skeletons

Keeping, Juliana. "Questions remain after discovery of bodies in Foss Lake," Online article, October 28, 2013.

Martinez, Michael. "Coroner: Remains from Oklahoma lake math genders, ages of six missing people," Online article CNN, October 13, 2013.

Ng, Christina. "Oklahoma Sunken Cars: Mysteries Solved for Families With Vanished Relatives," Online article, ABC NEWS, September 20, 2013.

Payne, Ed, Michael Martinez and ED Lavandera. "Oklahoma lake bodies: Diver, trooper recount discovery," Online article, CNN, September 19 2013.

Gone, But Not Very Far

Caron, Christina. "Skeleton Found in Chimney 27 years After Man Disappeared," Online article, July 27, 2011, ABCNEWS.

Foster, Mary. "Funeral for man entombed for 27 years in chimney," Online article, August 12, 2011, Yahoo News.

Two Who Vanished

"Bodies found in car in South Dakota creek are teens missing sine 1971," Reuters Media, Duluth News Tribune, April 15, 2014.

"Four decade mystery of missing South Dakota women solved," Online article, BBC NEWS-US & CANADA, April 16, 2014.

Pamela Jackson/Cheryl Miller, 1971, South Dakota – Cold Case Investigations, Online article, November 7, 2006. ""Bones found in farm search," September 9, 2004.

South Dakota girls missing since 1971 killed in car crash, officials say," Online article, Associated Press, April 16, 2014.

Young, Steve. "Families of missing girls yearn for closure," Online article, November 7, 2006.

Acknowledgments

Most notably, we are grateful to our family—Karen, Greg, and Dr. Arlene for their encouragement and support.

We thank David Misner who edited two stories in our book.

We appreciate the help we received from Rick Kerr, Lt. Colonel (ranger) U.S. Army (retired) who did the maps for the Ray Gricar and Bonnie & Mitchel stories. Rick also solved any computer problem that Harry has.

We thank Dr. Kirk Moll for doing the two USS Dorado maps.

We want to thank Dr. Martin Pastuka for his interest in our book.

We thank Dr. Diane Spokus, College of Health and Human Development at the Pennsylvania Sate University, for her steadfast support.

We appreciate the assistance we have received from the following at the Shippensburg University Library: Susan Hockenberry, Diane Kalathas, Mary Mowery, Teresa Strayer and Denise Wietry.

Our thanks to the following who have helped in one way or another: Kathy Brunie, Patricia Coia, Joann Grandi, Lucas and Jessica Kalathas, John,

Janine and Nick Kalathas, Carol Kerr (Col. USAR Ret.), John Kerr, 1st Lt. USAF, Katie Kerr, Rick Kerr, Capt. USAF and Rachel, Joseph and Cindy McAndrew, Stephanie Misner, Patrick, Nancy, Carrie Ann and Kathleen Shay.

A SPECIAL TRIBUTE

A time to remember the passing of Richard E. Kerr, Sr., a Korean War veteran, who served his country and family so well.

Proof

Made in the USA
Charleston, SC
30 December 2015